Finding You
Through
Finding Me

Cover Design Copyright © 2025 by Gabrielle Stone All rights reserved.
Cover Design by Murphy Rae, www.murphyrae.net
Back Cover Photography by Mija Kohlwey Photography
Edited by Ink Deep Editing
Formatting by Elaine York, Allusion Publishing, www.allusionpublishing.com
ISBN: 978-1-7339637-4-9

Come Play Online!
@gabriellestone
@taymourghazi

Finding You Through Finding Me

GABRIELLE STONE
& TAYMOUR GHAZI

Table of Contents

For anyone who's ever cried on the bathroom floor,
wondering if they'll ever feel complete.
For those who have questioned whether
they're unlovable.
For the people who feel like they just aren't enough.
For Juni.
For Stone.

Acknowledgements

This journey you're about to take will be fun and filled with humor—but please be aware there are more than a few heavy subjects addressed. If you have any triggers in the areas announced in the chapter titles, take care while reading.

We live in a strange time right now. Never has it been scarier to share opinions, take a stance, speak your mind, or, god forbid, say something where nuance is important. We are living in a time of cancellation. If you are reading this book, it is our hope that you will take what you need, understand our humor, and know that, just because we believe something (or not), that doesn't mean we cannot coexist. Art is subjective. Conversation is important. We welcome you to our world in hopes you will take this journey with us with an open mind and loving heart.

Gabs & Tay

Gabrielle

Well, hello there, friends. I'm sure some of you picked up this book because you've gone on some wild and crazy adventures with me. Others stumbled upon it by chance, which means this is absolutely where you're supposed to be. If you're the former, welcome back to the party. Admittedly, life is a little tamer these days than galivanting around Europe and Asia on life-changing solo adventures, dodging sociopathic ex-husbands, and navigating heartbreak on this complicated journey we call life. But lucky for you, this book is going to take you back to different times before I met the man I call my unicorn and lived happily ever after—because it was by no means a walk in the freaking park to get to fairy-tale land. In fact, that's really what this journey we're about to take you on is all about. How the hell did we stumble our way through life and end up with each other? Sure, soulmates and happy endings are cool and all, but have you ever woken up and felt: *Damn. I am so thankful for my life and everything in it. I feel so healed and so complete.* Trust me— it's better than any orgasm you'll ever have.

Let me tell you, there was a time I thought I would never get there. But not only is it possible, it is entirely *in your control.* When I approached my husband, Tay, about writing this book, it wasn't because I was dying to jump back into author mode—the thought of that is actually quite daunting and exhausting, particularly because I'm writing this with a newborn using my chest as a luxury pillow. It was because of how many messages I was getting from my heartbroken readers and podcast listeners asking the same question at the core: *How the hell do I find my person?* And to that, my response is simple: *Well, darling, I'm sure your person is out there, but have you even really found yourself?*

In addition to being for my single folks looking for answers, this book is also for those of you in a less-than-satisfying relationship, who feel like you settled or simply think you and the partner that you love have lost your way. It's amazing what can happen to a relationship in a rut when you finally begin to heal yourself. Our hope is that our journeys will guide you to whatever outcome is best for you— finding a path to fixing the relationship you're in, or giving you the courage to finally decide you're ready to leave.

It's not that you have to be fully healed or have it all figured out in order to attract the love you want in your life—or the career, friendships, or any other dreams you're wanting to create for yourself. But I promise you, it will come a hell of a lot easier if you've taken the time to learn the lessons your life has offered and have begun the process of really getting to know yourself.

The goal isn't to be perfect (because that doesn't exist) or magically healed (are we ever fully?) before *the one* bumps into you at a coffee shop and asks to take you on a romantic and spontaneous evening you'll never forget. The goal is to have done some of the work for *yourself*—and then continue to do the work once you guys are bingeing the third season of some terrible reality show while eating pizza in bed.

If you haven't yet read *Eat, Pray, #FML* and its sequel *The Ridiculous Misadventures of a Single Girl,* you'll get the CliffsNotes throughout different sections of this book. But the main thing you need to know is that—spoiler alert— in the end, I lived happily ever after and ended up with the man my readers now consider to be the standard below which you shouldn't settle. No pressure, babe. Can't wait for my audience to meet you.

Tay will probably undersell himself at the start of this book, saying he isn't the writer in the relationship. Let me give you a heads-up—that is bullshit. I can assure you, I wouldn't ask someone to co-write a book with me who wasn't going to deliver in the same way I do. He is a true Renaissance man, and, if anything, he'll have to scale back his beautifully poetic sentences and add a few f-bombs to match what my readers have come to love and expect from me. Really, what I'm most excited for you all to experience is a real, authentic, emotional, and soul-baring account of a human's journey...from the man I, and so many of my readers, have come to love. The person that made me realize it was never going to work with anyone else. The person I was waiting to find.

But finding Tay wasn't something that happened because I paid my dues, or got lucky, or even because I deserved to find a man like him. I found Tay because I found myself first. Because I did the work to heal what was within *me*. And even then, something magical *still* had to happen on the other end of it all. *He* had to heal and find himself on his own. Because only then, when two people truly have gone on their journeys, can they say:

I found you through finding me.

Taymour

Well...Where do I even begin? Should I start with the *I'm not the writer of the family* intro or just hit you hard with *Look, we just had a baby fifteen days ago and are still gonna try and write this freaking book* intro? Here, how about this...

Allow me to introduce myself. My name is Taymour Ghazi. My friends call me Tay. Some of you have come here by way of my wife Gabrielle Stone's wonderful books. Through her jaw-dropping, chest-opening roller coaster of a few years spread out amongst some 600 pages. If you have come from that avenue, I guess now is as good of a time as any to throw out a spoiler alert: Yes, I am Tyler. And yes, we fucking made it. And WHOA, what a journey it was. If you haven't already, I highly suggest giving them a read, as Gabrielle pens her journey elaborately and eloquently, with enough detail to understand her trials and tribulations throughout. Her journey is so relatable it is hard not to evaluate your own life choices while reading.

She and countless others, including myself, have traveled through life either searching for "the one" or settling for the "wrong one." For the longest time I looked and wondered, *What is it that some others have that we don't? And why do I see all these damn couples just fucking thriving in all of their disgusting happiness?* After years of experiencing life as it comes and discovering myself in the process, I came to the glaring realization that the people who were fully happy in their relationships were fully happy with themselves. Their self-love was through the roof. It was undeniable. And that was something that I just did not possess. I was reckless with my self-love and I was reckless with my self-care. It wasn't until I fully loved myself that I was able to fully love someone else and, moreover, receive their love of me. It's a wicked conundrum that only clears itself with life experience and the motivation to actually put *yourself* first. It's an expedition I have been on for over a decade and foresee myself being on for the remainder of my life. I mean, self-love? Like putting yourself first and shit? Fine. No problem. Count me in.

When Gabrielle first came up with the idea for us to write a book together, I loved it, but I quickly realized the daunting responsibility I would have to anyone who would read it. My wife has a wonderful audience of mostly women who have followed her journey from the beginning through two books and now a successful podcast. She is empowering thousands of women to make a change, choose themselves first, and begin on a path of self-love, all of which is a necessity to living a healthy, happy life and, most of all, finding healthy love. Although I may have discovered that secret through some rough days of my own, it wasn't until I was with Gabrielle that I firmly began to realize it. But how could I contribute to the message? How could I empower women and men alike through my words? I knew the answer to be simple and true. Transparency. I would just need to tell my story with all its blunders, hiccups, birthday cakes, and checkered flags. And just like that, that daunting responsibility felt like a magical opportunity.

Maybe if I told my story in conjunction with Gabrielle's, people would see *our* through line. Maybe they'd find a connection to their own story. And, perhaps, make a change. Or just enjoy our journey. It was a win-win and made perfect sense. Before long, we had enough shit for ten books. There's a lot of life lived between us. If you do the math, it's over eighty years. But who the fuck likes math? And yes, I'm older than you think. But seriously, we've lived lives filled to the brim with all the trimmings life holds. A lot of happiness and sadness, tragedy and triumph. Love, death, broken hearts, achieved dreams, and everything in between. Life has been a circus one night and a black-tie ball another. I've cried in the same exact day that I've laughed until I peed myself...true story. I've sat in my lowest valleys and embraced them, and I've stopped to appreciate the high peaks. I fucking LOVE life. Even when it's not that great. There...I said it.

Through all the ups and downs and happy and sad moments, when Gabrielle became a consistent presence in my life, everything began to shift slightly and then fall into place. But why? Why then? Why her? And therein lies the through line of this book. How discovering, healing, and loving ourselves made us ready to give ourselves to another. If you are like me, you've been through numerous relationships, some magical and some horrific. But in them all, regardless of duration or meaning, there was always a purpose. Always a lesson. I am a serial monogamist (more on that later), and I realized at a young age that I was always searching. For what, I didn't know, nor did I possess the life experience to know. But then I did the work, learned the lessons, and came to the glaringly obvious realization—*I was searching to find myself.*

Oh, the paths I've walked. The sights I've seen. I've been through tragedy. I've walked the dark halls of addiction. I've experienced the pains of divorce, and the severity of loneliness. Life is not always the metaphorical bowl of cherries some speak of. I'm a proud father to an absolutely incredible daughter, and now, a wonderfully magical new son. I have made a thousand and one mistakes in my life— and I will probably make a few hundred more. But I am still here to tell you about each and every one. To tell my daughter and my son that I am human. To search and search to find that better self inside of me. Always and forever.

So, here we go....

Loss of a Parent

"Those we love never truly leave us.
There are things that death cannot touch."
– Harry Potter

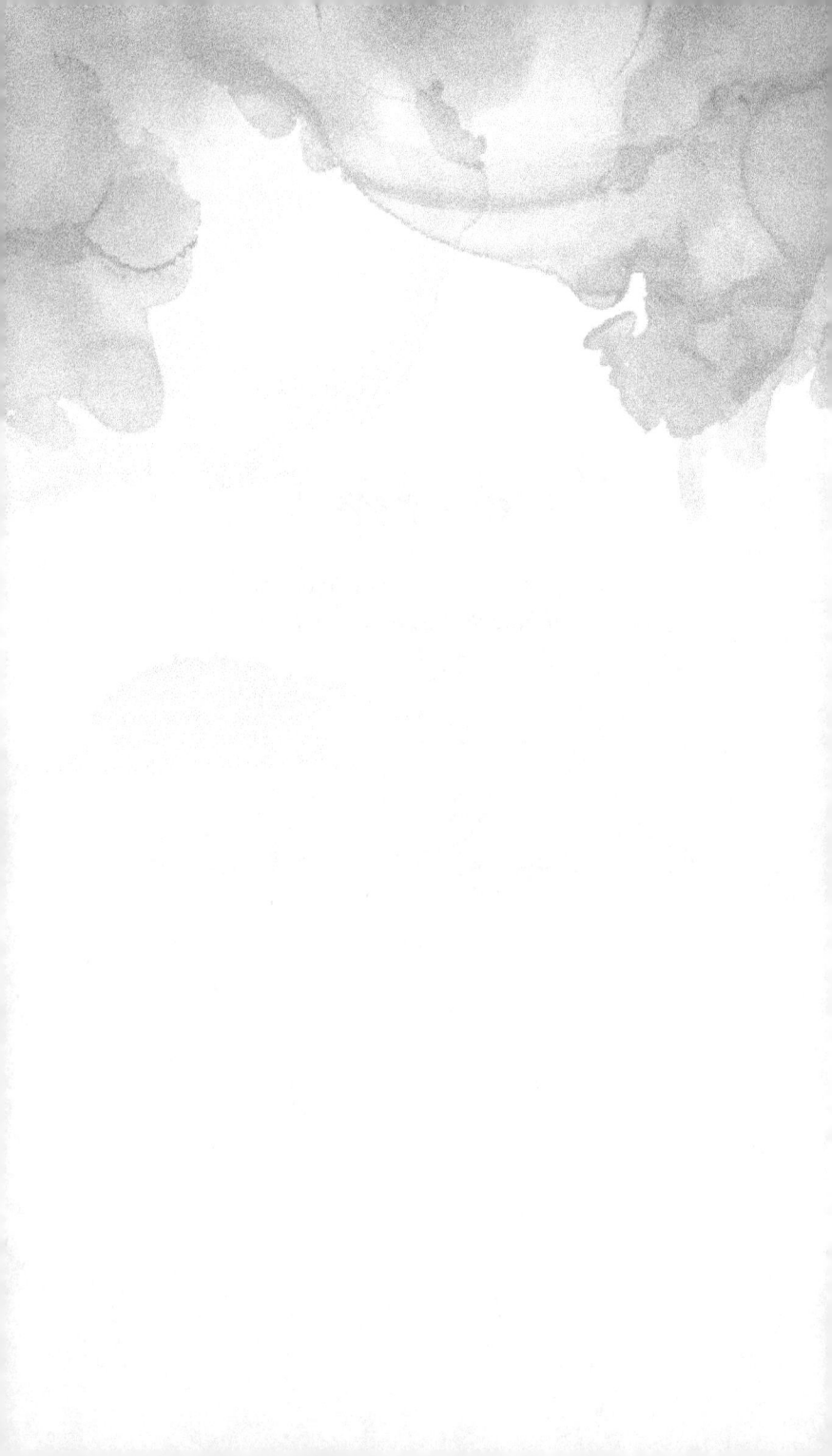

Gabrielle

I don't know what is worse. Losing someone when you're young, before you have time to get to know them as an adult, to fall in love with their spirit, to fear life without them. Or losing someone later in life, when all those magical feelings have imbedded themselves deep inside your heart. Which is more heartbreaking? Which brings more grief? I don't have an answer to this question. I've experienced both, but this first story is about a loss that happened far too early, before my young heart even knew about this thing they call death. Before I realized I should fear life without him...before I knew how truly fleeting life can be.

My father was my hero. At least in my little six-year-old mind he was. Later in life, I would find out that the big burly marine and ex-Hollywood playboy never really envisioned himself as a dad. But you know what they say, it only takes the perfect wholesome blonde from Kansas City to change that. My dad fell for my mom like all the great love stories of our time. He found her home address and sent her flowers before she got home on the day they met on set. You know, what we consider stalker behavior in today's world.

Even now, three decades after his untimely death, many relationships and a marriage later, it is known by all that they were the true definition of soulmates. And because he had met his soulmate, my dad suddenly changed his tune and decided to become a father.

My mother, on the other hand, always wanted to be a mom. Even when her body said, "No bitch, this ain't in the cards for you," and handed her the biggest fibroid tumor on record at the time, she laughed, and responded, "That's hilarious. The universe and I have other plans." Every doctor and specialist told her to give up. I mean, after all, she was already (GASP) *FORTY*—and it was the eighties. No one was having kids at forty in the eighties. So, after six long years of her trying to will a child into this world, I finally made my grand entrance. (I say grand because after twenty-four hours in labor, you deserve the 'grand' title.)

I came out screaming bloody murder, as most babies do. (How rude to take us out of a dark comfy slumber, slap us on the ass, poke and prod at us, and then expect us to just be cute and darling.) Once I was cleaned up, my dad leaned over the table I was on. He began to hum "Life is Just a Bowl of Cherries," which is what he would sing to my mom's pregnant belly. I stopped screaming, looked up toward him, and reached my miniature hand in his direction. The nurses all cried. It was very Hallmark. And just like that, he became wrapped around my tiny finger. I was daddy's little girl.

Six years seems like a long time when you're waiting for a promotion. Six years feels like the blink of an eye when you're traveling the world. We didn't know it, but that is all we had. Six years to get to know each other, to fall in love with each other's spirit, to fear life without one another. Well, at least *I* didn't know it...

In his early twenties, my dad saw a psychic reader (guess this theme runs in the family) who was wildly accurate about a lot of things in his life. She told him that he would die of natural causes right before his fifty-fifth birthday. He died on October 20th when he was fifty-four. Moral of the story? When a psychic asks you if you want to know *all* the information, no matter what, be careful what your answer is.

My dad was no stranger to death. In his early thirties he had dropped to the floor from a brain aneurysm, where he remained for two days until a friend found him. People rarely survive aneurysms (which you'll hear about in Tay's experience) but somehow, when he got to the hospital, he was still hanging on. Years later he would tell the story of what he experienced that day:

All of a sudden, I was up in the top corner of the operating room, looking down at my body. I could see all the doctors and nurses working on me. I turned away from the scene below me and saw a beautiful bright light. It felt like the most peaceful, wonderful feeling imaginable. It was euphoria. I wanted to go toward it. Then, I had the thought: 'I feel like there's something I still have left to do...' and BAM. I woke up in my body two days later without a scratch or scar on me.

Obviously, that something was me. I mean, hello, not to pull the *only child, center of attention* card, but I'm kind of a big deal. Kidding, of course, but I do believe in soul contracts (please see FML Talk podcast season 5 episode #4), and my father and I definitely had some karmic contracts to fulfill before he peaced out back to the other side. And besides, he totally had to have the greatest love affair of his life and lose his player ways before he went on to his next big adventure.

To fully grasp one of the through lines of this book, it is important to note that Christopher Stone, my dad, became a father at the age of forty-eight. My husband Tay was forty-nine when we had our son. Coincidence? Ha...there is no such thing. We'll circle back to this revelation a bit later.

To me, my dad was invincible. He was strong, an ex-marine, charismatic, and dashingly good-looking. Through my six-year-old eyes, he was absolutely unstoppable. Now, as an adult, I can look at photos over the years and see how quickly he was aging and that his health was secretly declining.

My parents were both in the entertainment industry. When they had me, they made a rule that if one of them took a job, the other parent wouldn't. Furthermore, if one parent was out of town for longer than a week for a project, the whole family would go. This is wildly difficult to do in such a *take the jobs as they come* type industry, but it meant sometimes Dad and I were at home with Mom away, and sometimes vice versa. This particular time, it was Mom's turn away.

She was in New Zealand filming a movie called *The Frighteners,* and Kristen (my nanny) and I had just returned home from two weeks in that beautiful country with Mom on set. Back home with Dad, I begged him to take me to the park to play baseball. That was our thing—baseball. He would take me to the Angels games, and I knew all the players' names. I was also the only girl on my baseball team. He told me he was tired but I persisted, so he, Kristen, and I loaded up and headed to the park a few miles away. We threw some balls back and forth, and I hit a few he pitched to me, but then he sat down to take a breather.

"What's going on?" Kristen asked him, noticing something was off.

"I just have heartburn or something," he said, drinking a soda and trying to burp.

Kristen and I kept playing. He didn't get up.

"You sure you're okay?" she asked again.

"I don't know..." he said, pressing his chest.

"We're leaving. Decide if we're going home or to the hospital," she said to him. "Let's go, Gaby!" she called to me from the side of the field.

"But we just got here!" My six-year-old self failed to read the room.

"We'll come back tomorrow, baby," she said.

"Why don't you drive," my dad said to her. Kristen suddenly realized something was very wrong. Dad didn't ever ask her to drive. She hopped in the driver's seat and pulled toward the parking lot exit.

"Take a right." He pointed. We weren't going home. We were going to the hospital.

Now, for most men, shit has to be *serious* for them to admit that there is something wrong and willingly go to the doctor or hospital. Kristen knew damn well that something must be going on.

That something was a heart attack.

Mom was on the next flight home. The journey from New Zealand to Los Angeles is roughly fourteen hours with a massive time difference to adjust to. She arrived, took care of me, and then headed to the hospital to check on my dad.

"I'm fine. Seriously, the doctors are letting me go home tomorrow. You need to go back and finish the film."

After a few days at home, witnessing my dad on the mend, and some extra convincing, my mom headed back to New Zealand to do just that. If "finish what you started" was a human, it would be my mother. Everything seemed fine for a few days—and then it happened.

Those of you who read *Eat, Pray, #FML* got the CliffsNotes version of the way my six-year-old brain remembered the events that took place that day. What I am about to take you through is what my adult self now knows to be true.

I woke up on a Saturday, excited to spend the day watching cartoons in bed with Dad, who was still resting and recovering. Kristen had made me promise to wait until 11 a.m. to go in and wake him up, so we had breakfast and played while I waited anxiously. When the clock struck 10:59, I raced into his bedroom and was surprised to find his bed empty. I crossed through the room around the king-size bed and into my parents' master bathroom. There was my dad, lying face down on the carpeted floor. I ran back through the bedroom and into the dining room, yelling, "Kristen, Kristen, Daddy passed out!"

I have a vivid flash memory in my brain of Kristen FLYING by me in the dining room and into the bedroom, where I followed.

"STAY THERE," she said to me as she reached the bathroom.

Kristen came back out, took me back to my bedroom, and turned on the TV. She then called 911.

"I don't want anything to be wrong with Daddy. I want him to be okay."

"I know, honey, me too." She held my tiny self in her big, tight grasp.

One of the paramedics walked into the doorway of my room as I was still hugging Kristen, my back to him. He looked at her with a look that said everything we were both hoping not to hear—then mouthed, *You have to tell her.*

Kristen then did what I can only imagine was one of the hardest things she had done in a very long time. She told a six-year-old girl that her daddy was dead. We cried. We hugged. We cried some more.

Then she called my mom.

"What's wrong?" My mom's intuition must have answered the phone that day. "Is Gaby okay?"

"Gaby's alright."

"What's wrong?"

"Christopher's gone," Kristen said.

"What?" She couldn't comprehend.

"Christopher's gone," she repeated.

"What?"

"He's dead, Dee."

She needed to hear the actual words. She needed to know that her biggest fear was actually happening. Let's take a moment to put ourselves in my mom's shoes. Not only was the love of her life now gone, she was across the world and had received the news that, on top of all this, her daughter had been the one to find him. It makes my heart hurt for her just thinking about it.

My mother, ever the warrior that she is, immediately went into damage-control mode. So often when we see movies where someone is told devastating news, they drop to their knees, let out a guttural scream, and begin to hysterically cry. In reality, often our bodies go into complete and utter shock—and our brain shuts off emotions so that we can manage our way through the situation. This was one of those times.

"Where's Gaby?" she immediately asked.

"She's in her room. I can see her from where I'm standing."

"Put her on the phone."

We spoke. About what, I don't remember. What do you say to your six-year-old daughter who doesn't really understand what the hell death even is? How do you explain that her father is no longer here, even though he's lying on the bathroom floor? I don't envy anyone that is faced with that daunting task—especially from halfway around the world.

"I'm sorry to have to ask you to do this," my mom said to Kristen after I had handed the phone back to her, "but I need you to take Gabrielle in to say goodbye to her daddy. I need her to know that she doesn't need to be afraid."

"Okay, Dee. Of course." Kristen was only twenty-two years old. Let *that* sink in for a second.

Now, as traumatic as this all sounds, I need to point out how incredibly thankful I am that my mom made this decision. That moment, that time she gave me with him, whether my brain blocked it out or disassociated at the time, did something monumentally important. In that moment, subconsciously, two things happened. One, I was able to see and believe that Daddy was gone. I saw a body and I knew that he was no longer in there. The dots connected in my little brain. Twelve years later, when my high school sweetheart died in a car crash, I didn't go and see the body. I can confirm from the random dreams and the moments where I see what looks like him on the freeway, my brain *did not* connect those dots. For years a part of me felt like... *but is he really dead? Or is everyone just fucking with me?*

The other thing this did was allow me to truly say goodbye. Kristen placed her hand on my dad's lifeless body.

"See, Gaby. It's still Daddy. He's just gone to a different place now. Do you want to tell him anything?"

"I love you, Daddy," I said with tears on my tiny cheeks. Even now as I write this, twenty-nine years later, my eyes are just a little bit wet. For the longest time, I had absolutely no memory of this. In my mind, I went to my room, turned on the TV, then heard the ambulance sirens. When I first discovered him, I had thought he had simply fainted. But when I went back into that room, I knew I was walking into a space with a body of a person who was no longer inside of it. After many years, and recounting the story with both Kristen and my mom, my brain has begun to allow that memory back in. It's present now, after being locked away for my protection for a very long time. I can now see him, in his pajama bottoms and Dodgers shirt, lying on the floor as I said goodbye.

My mom was on the next flight home. As security was escorting her to the front of the customs line, a frustrated traveler stepped to the side and shouted, "Hey! Why does she get to cut the line?"

My mom stopped, turned to him with tears in her eyes, and said, "Because my husband just died, and my little girl needs me."

If you haven't realized by this point, let me make it clear: *My mom is superwoman.* She arrived home, took care of me, got his affairs in order, and had my dad's celebration of life. Then, a few days after her soulmate died, she put me and Kristen back on a plane with her and flew back to finish the fucking film. If you think I was brave for taking a month-long solo trip to Europe after some asshole broke my heart... it's only because life threw my mother a grief bomb and my mother said, *Hold my beer.* We landed in New Zealand, she took a shower, *and went straight back to set.*

This fateful day. This trauma. This tragedy. This *experience.* At the ripe age of six years old, my life was forever changed. Whether I knew it at that moment or not, life bestowed on me the first big scar that I would need to find a way to heal. And unbeknownst to me, it would be the biggest healing lesson of my life. When a massive event happens in your life, a belief is left behind. For me, this first belief was as simple as my little six-year-old brain. *When I love someone, they die.* At the core of that belief is the fear of abandonment. How would I ever find peace in a relationship if I was in constant fear of that person leaving... or worse, dying? The answer to that is unfortunately (for me) very dark and unhealthy. I would attract men into my life that would, in a variety of ways, abandon me. Strap in, guys, it's a long freaking road to heal from those beliefs that imbed themselves in our brains at such a young age. But I promise you—by the end of this book, we will reach our destination.

I don't know if you ever truly heal from the death of a parent—or any important death, for that matter. What I do know is that what they say is true. Time really does *help* all. Between losing my dad and my high school sweetheart, death and grief have not been strangers in my life. We've met, had tea, and I got the stupid T-shirt. Yet, with all the death throughout the years, what once felt like a gaping, bleeding wound now feels like a scar that reminds me of the life I've lived. There is a peace I find in knowing and believing that there is something beyond this physical realm—because those who have left me here on earth have sent me far too many signs to think anything else.

When I first met Tay, I was terrified. He was, after all, a mirror for all the things I was afraid of. He was just like my dad—charming, strong, charismatic—and he had a little girl that was the exact age I was when I lost my father. So, of course, I couldn't date him, because he would *obviously* die on me. Although these fears resurfacing brought new things for me to work through, I ultimately did—*because* of what I had learned from losing my dad.

Live. In the end, the biggest lesson it taught me is *to live.* Live like tomorrow isn't promised. Explore like it's your last adventure on earth. Cherish like it's the last hug. And love like they could be gone tomorrow. I think I subconsciously learned this from watching my mother as that little girl. I continued to learn it with my firsthand experience of how unfairly fleeting life can be, which you'll read about in the next chapter. And finally, as an adult, I was reminded yet again by my mother when she so eloquently said, "Gabrielle, you could get hit by a bus tomorrow. Who cares that he's fifteen years older."

If I hadn't learned that lesson so early, and been consistently faced with obstacles to heal around it, who knows if I would have run the other way when I met Tay. Even now that he's my husband and the father of my child, I still have to remind myself that *he is here*. Whether it is for another week, another year, another decade, or more. And when the fear of losing him creeps in, I remind myself how deeply my mother cherishes the twenty years she had with my dad—and wouldn't have it any other way.

My mom and Kristen taught me that day that death isn't something scary. It is sad and often unfair and untimely, but it isn't something haunting that should be feared. Death is a natural part of life—and I fully believe that what comes after death is nothing short of magical. I know that my dad, as much as he didn't *want* to leave me, finally got to go experience that beautiful white light that had called his name over twenty years before. I know one day my mom will be swept up into her soulmate's arms yet again. And I know one day, hopefully long from now, I will sit with both of them, looking down, and watch my son carry on, as we all have carried on, with the bits and pieces he's collected from everyone who has come before him.

Taymour

It would be ignorant to think that experiences don't shape us—so I don't do that. We are reflections of our experiences, whether traumatic or triumphant. Some of those experiences we'd like to forget and some are memorialized with trophies in our rooms. Regardless of worth, these experiences shape us, and the sooner we realize that, the sooner we can heal from the experiences that hurt.

Let me paint the picture for you. I grew up in Marin County, a northern suburb of the San Francisco Bay Area. Although the location was a mix between middle and upper class, it was mostly upper class. We fell smack dab in between the two classes. My immigrant father owned, and still owns to this day, the oldest bar in San Francisco called The Little Shamrock. (Fun fact: He bought the bar the day I was born on his way home from the hospital...with a bad check he quickly covered from a loan via his new father-in-law.) We had enough money to support where we lived and how we lived, but I do remember many arguments that turned into fights about money and the struggles that come along with it. I learned from a young age that life should not revolve around money—it should revolve around love and family. We were a very happy family, even when we were struggling financially. When I say happy, I really mean it. It was my mom, my dad, and me for the first ten years of my life, and then my brother, Tavahn, was a welcome addition. Life was great when I was a kid. My dad was my soccer coach. My mom kept the house. Everything was peacefully balanced and everyone was happy. My parents were young and energetic, having had me at thirty years old. I remember at an early age wanting to emulate the life they provided me with. Not so much the white picket fence, cookie-cutter family picture, but just the young, vibrant energy that both my parents brought to the table. It made me want to have a family. It made me want to be a parent. And now, being a parent two times over, I look back on some of the morals, ideals, and family values that were instilled in me at such a young age, and see a direct link to my two children. It's beautiful to see, and I am forever grateful for that genealogy.

Just as in every family, there is far more to the story than just rainbows and unicorn shit. I will go into more detail in other parts of the book, but for the sake of this chapter I will leave it here—there was no shortage of fire in our household. My parents could love like the best of 'em, but they could also fight like the best of them. And to say that it didn't shape me or leave an impact would be a downright lie. But for the most part, I was happy, energetic, and thriving. I had a great group of friends and an amazing family, and I was shaping up to be the happiest kid on the planet. The operative word there being *shaping*. You see, the real shaping of my existence was right around the corner and I was about to be blindsided by it. All the love, all the happiness and fun and joyful madness that was our family drastically changed in the blink of an eye. I remember the day like it was yesterday. As I get older, sure, memories begin to fade, but for some reason those few fateful days will never leave. Funny how trauma works.

It was April 17th, 1988. It was a beautiful Sunday morning, and I was all pissed off. I was thirteen years old, and the group of friends that I had been running around with since kindergarten were getting together for a swim party. I wanted to go, but no, my mother had other plans. Her grand romantic plan was for the family to do the most dreaded, most miserable, awful thing for any thirteen-year-old to partake in—*yard work*. Now, make no mistake about it, I was a fun, energetic teen that was extremely respectful to everyone around me...*except my mother*. I don't know what it was about our dynamic, but boy oh boy did we fight. It was a constant battle. My mom was a tough cookie, but looking back (and now being a parent), I have to take the blame for a lot of it. I was extremely sensitive and suffered the only-child syndrome big time. My brother was ten years younger than me, and before he joined the crew I was a spoiled little shit. So, suffice it to say, it was my mother that led the charge in shaping me up. And on this fateful day, I was not having it. After breakfast and another healthy argument about me going to my friend's house, we began the day's work. To say that I was pissed off is an understatement. I was looking for a fight. A few hours into what any teen would deem hell on earth— raking a field of damp fresh-cut grass—my mom and I were passing through a narrow entryway in our garage and we bumped into each other. I probably laid a little more shoulder into that bump than was appropriate. I certainly had the potential to be a dick at times. She grabbed me rather violently by the arm, and through gritted teeth she threatened, "I'm your mother, you'll treat me with respect." I yanked my arm from her grip and grinned at her. In the fifty years that

I have been alive, I have never wanted to take back words as much as I wanted to take back what I said to her in that moment. In fact, the words that came out of my mouth quite literally changed my life forever—for so many reasons that are littered throughout the pages of this book. It was this day, it was this moment, that my life forever took a different course.

I hate you and I wish you were dead.

She stared at me with such a look of defeat, almost as if she knew right then. There was a dramatic moment of silence that I'll never forget. All she could muster up before sullenly walking off was, "One of these days, you're going to regret those words. I'm sorry."

I'm sorry? Sorry for what? She had to end it with I'm sorry? I can still hear her voice. Why did she say she was sorry? It was so weird and out of context at the time. My young self was just annoyed and wanted to get out of there. I remember walking away being so enraged, but that rage quickly turned to a bitter sadness. Sadness that I had said something like that. Let me be clear, my mother and I had a tumultuous relationship at times, but we loved each other deeply, and when we weren't fighting, I did show her the utmost respect. We were very close. So when those words came out of my mouth, I knew I had fucked up. I regretted them immediately but was too stubborn to apologize. My teenage hormones decided that silence was my remedy. We went about our day, finishing the grueling yard work, mad as hell. Not a single word was exchanged between us for the rest of...well...*her life*.

After my shower, I planned on staying in my room in protest until dinner. My dad hopped in the shower with my stinky little brother, and I figured my mom was probably smoking a cigarette on the side yard. According to my dad, about ten minutes later he began calling for my mom to retrieve my brother from the shower. No response. Again and again with no response. He finally yelled for me to go find her. I went right to where I thought she would be—and sure enough, there she was. Lying face up with her eyes open. A sobering wave of shock washed over me. I froze.

Annnd...cue the sudden wild rush of guilt on my thirteen-year-old psyche. *Did I just wish my mom dead?* But there was no time to ponder. I jumped into action. I sprinted through the house and slammed the bathroom door open, screaming, "MOM IS DEAD. COME QUICK!" My dad shrieked something fierce and came barreling out of the shower. En route through the kitchen, he came in so hot he almost ended his own life. Soaking wet, he slid across the tile floor and into the wall, nearly breaking his neck. It really was horrific to see. While my dad ran to my mom, I rushed to the phone and dialed 9-1-1. It was my first time calling 9-1-1, and I am hoping my very last. It was frantic and I can't remember much of it. Something along the lines of "my mom is dead" and "get here fast." I was answering their questions when all of a sudden, sure as shit, here comes my four-year-old brother, soaking wet and naked, chasing my dad and giggling, thinking we were playing some sort of weird game. I mean, can you blame him? He was almost four and just saw Dad jump out of the shower and start running. He was already precocious, so this was right up his alley. As tragic as that day was, I have to look back on this one moment and laugh. Poor kiddo just doing his best to have fun without knowing the true nature of the beast.

In under one minute, the EMTs were there, doing whatever they could to keep her alive. Once they arrived, my dad stayed with them, while I wrangled my brother. Luckily, in all of the hysterics, he didn't escape and wander off to discover the sight that is forever burned in my brain. Within a few minutes time they were whisking her out into an ambulance while all of our neighbors looked on in horror. Our closest neighbor, my mother's best friend, Linda, came to the rescue with her three daughters and took my brother with them while my father and I went to the hospital. We still had no idea what was going on. Was it a heart attack? A stroke? After a series of tests, we received the most severe news possible—my mom had collapsed from an irreversible brain aneurysm about fifteen minutes after we were done with the stupid, fucking yard work. There was no avoiding it. We had found her in time to keep her alive, but her brain function was at a zero. We would never have my mom back ever again. And with that news came the daunting task of having to decide whether to pull the plug on her life or have her remain in the care of machines.

It was a heavy decision that no child should ever have a vote in, but there was no way my dad was going to make that decision alone. I saw it in his eyes. After all the questions were answered, I softly said, "We have to do it." So we did.

My mom died April 21st, 1988. She was surrounded by most of her loved ones prior to stopping the machines. I stood there, watching, drowning in a terrible sinkhole of guilt. I not only had to make the final decision to pull the plug and face the loss of my mother, I also had to reckon with the last words I had spoken to her. Remember how I said my life changed for a few reasons with the loss of my mother? Well, that guilt was the main one. I carried it around like a sadistic badge of honor for years after. That guilt was the catalyst for many life decisions that I still question to this day. It was also responsible for struggles with addiction, fighting, and strained relationships. I held onto that guilt for far longer than it was welcome. I didn't take the proper steps to repair the wound that guilt left... and I didn't take the proper steps to repair the wound of losing my mother.

Guilt to me is kind of like a leech that you can't see or touch but you know it's there, just slowly sucking the life out of you. I have come to realize that when I hold onto guilt, or anything that I feel doesn't allow me to progress, I struggle to find myself and in turn struggle to love myself. When I look back on my life, the times I was most angry and unsettled was when I was holding on to heavy things like guilt. And therein lies the through line of this book. How can one love anyone else completely when they don't love themself? When they haven't given enough attention to the guilt or regret or other hindrance that isn't allowing them to progress? They just sweep it under the rug and hope it magically goes away. It doesn't. It creeps up on you like an unstoppable force and leads to drastically poor life decisions. I wish I would've been privy to the slippery slope guilt creates, but I certainly don't regret it. Because of that slippery slope I'm now able to ski. See what I did there? No, but really, I have come to accept the bad with the good. I'm hoping I have become intelligent enough to learn the lessons when available and to process failure or mistakes as a crucial element to existence. The jury's still out.

The loss of a parent is tragic beyond belief. There is no way around that fact. It completely shaped me and still shapes me as I continue to evolve. It left an indelible impact on my life in so many ways. It taught me at an early age that life is utterly and unforgivingly delicate. That we need to live in each moment and cherish it. Love each moment until it passes and then begin to love the next. And the people in your life? Hug them just a little longer and take a moment to tell them how much they mean to you. After my mom died, I became a massive hugger and someone who was forthright with my emotions because I walked around with the fear that others too would just up and die on me. That fear stemmed from a young boy's loss, but I soon began to realize that I could not fear death, rather I had to respect it. Respect it and embrace each day as if it were my last. All these things began to change my outlook on life and my outlook on myself. Don't get me wrong, I was still severely sad and not properly mourning my mother's death, but I was also changing as a person at every turn—and changing for the better. I was beginning to embrace my feelings and express my emotions more freely. With the guilt and abandonment pinching me at every turn, I started to develop a new appreciation for life. It sounds contradictory, but I eventually began to process the guilt and abandonment and lean into that new appreciation. And that appreciation led to me loving myself just a little more.

I miss my mom. I wish I could go back and let her know how sorry I am for what I said—but I know she knows. I feel that and I have forgiven myself. And now she lives through me and my brother in so many distinct ways...and it's beautiful. She was gorgeous in every way, and I hold her very close to all of my life choices. She was my pillar, and I will forever stand a little tilted without her. Those who have the vacancy of a parent in their heart know this all too well.

Unfortunately, it is much the same for my better half. She too has been dealt a different hand than most with the loss of her father at a young age. And now that so many years have passed, I actually cherish that similarity. Albeit somewhat morbid, the shared experience we have has become comforting. We share some of the same abandonment issues that losing a parent so generously provides but, because of that similarity, we are able to harness each other's hearts when hurting. It is a common bond that no one wants to share, but if processed correctly it can be the remedy to a lot of suffering.

For me, it really comes down to my children now. The loss of my mother was tragic, but I have shifted my grief over into creating as much life as possible for my kids. I'm not gonna lie. I've never feared my own death as much as I have recently. Not because I'm scared to die, but because of the fear of my children experiencing the same exponential loss that Gabrielle and I did. So my focus is clear. The plan is laid. Live long, live happy, and live healthy, and walk hand in hand with my wife and kids until my wife and I are being taken care of by them. And if, for some deeper reason, a soul has to leave before the rest of us are ready...I know we will all be okay. After all, I was.

First Love

"First love can break you. But it can also save you."
– Katie Kahn

Gabrielle

My first love was also my first big heartbreak. That sounds totally typical. Obviously, when your young heart first opens its gates to someone, the most probable outcome is for the gates to be slammed shut and your heart to be broken. I mean, we still have so much to learn at the ripe age of seventeen. Unfortunately, my heartbreak was far from typical, and my gates weren't slammed, they were shattered. Because my first love didn't cheat, or break up with me on the football field, or pressure me at prom...my first love died.

I've talked and written only very briefly about this relationship—partly because it was so very long ago, and partly because it's always felt so deeply personal. It was, after all, not only my first love but the catalyst for so many different healings. But before we get into the myriad ways this tragic event rippled throughout my life, let me take you back to the best summer of my carefree teenage years in 2005...the summer before junior year.

Josh was the ultimate bad boy who, on the inside, was the most sensitive person I'd ever met. He drove a big black truck with the saying *Live The Life* plastered across it. It roared when he pulled into the school parking lot, and he'd hop out with his lip piercing and effortlessly cool skater-vibe wardrobe. He was Ryan Atwood from *The O.C.* in real life—and I was *smitten*.

Funny enough, the first time we hung out, we were making out with other people, side by side on my bed. (Sorry, Mom.) I vividly remember opening my eyes from the god-awful make-out sesh I was enduring with his friend, locking eyes with him (while he was making out with some random girl who was clearly not important enough to remember,) and thinking, *God, I wish I was making out with him instead.*

Turned out, he had the exact same thought running through his head. The next Monday at school, he handed me a note during passing period. By the end of junior year, I had a box full of them. We would write back and forth to each other constantly...because who the hell is paying attention to the overly complicated math I will clearly never be using. While we're on the subject (no pun intended), I wish schools would start teaching shit we actually *need* in life. Would love to know how to properly do my taxes, make smart investments, and, you know, purchase a home...but by all means, teach me about that one random battle that happened over a century ago and triga-whatever the hell it's called. They have really served me so far in life. Anyway...I digress.

I'll never forget the day at nutrition break when he came over, grabbed the note I had written him, and offered me his jacket. It was a black windbreaker that had a big white spade on it and said West Coast or some (now) really lame but (then) knee-weakening cool saying. I wore it to my next period, taking giant inhales of his Acqua Di Gio cologne probably a bit too often, and suddenly noticed them for the first time: *butterflies.*

There's something special about the first time you get big butterflies. I'd had a few boyfriends in the past, some serious relationships (I mean, as serious as you can be in high school), and those had their moments and a few butterflies here and there. This was entirely different. This was a Niagara Falls amount of butterflies, spilling into my stomach like the roaring water, making it completely impossible to focus on anything else. This...was puppy love.

Even Josh's ex-girlfriend was cool. She went to a different school than us, so I did a thorough stalking on her MySpace and Live Journal (how far back did *that* just jolt you?) to see what the previous girl was like. She was so cool. Her name was Genesis, and she too drove a big silver truck with some (now) lame but (then) very cool saying across the side. She had piercings, a tattoo, dark olive skin, and bright green eyes. Their style, their vibe, it all matched...

I was a blonde cheerleader.

After Josh and I had become boyfriend and girlfriend, there were rumors that Genesis was jealous and wanted him back. I distinctly remember getting ready in my room one day and having the thought (trigger warning), *If he breaks up with me, I'll just kill myself.* Dramatic much, Gabrielle? Jesus. Welcome to being a girl in high school who is going through puberty and entirely out of touch with reality. Happy to report that, although Genesis (who I became good friends with later) did indeed try to get him back, the blonde cheerleader prevailed, and I didn't have to go through with my *Romeo and Juliet* fiasco.

This relationship was the first of what my mother would call my "bad boy phase." That phase was as it sounds, but it also meant boys (this eventually became men) that I had to *fix*. Whether they had past trauma, a history of cheating, or just didn't have their shit together, I volunteered as tribute to fix them. And fix them I did.

When I started dating Josh, he was not only a huge stoner, he was also the main weed dealer in the Valley. I *think* my mother is aware of this now but has probably blocked it out of her memory so, yet again, sorry, Mom. He smoked about a half a pack of Parliament Lights a day which (now) makes me want to vomit in my mouth but (then) was so incredibly bad-boy sexy. Ah, the things we find exciting in our youth.

We had the most epic summer. We went to all the parties together, where I felt so beyond cool to be *his* girlfriend. Spent days on the beach with his senior friends. Took a trip to Palm Springs, went to the desert to ride ATVs with his family, and did what teenagers in high school do—have lots of steamy make-out sessions...and lots of sex.

That's not to say our relationship was perfect. I mean, hello, did you hear my dramatic intrusive thought a few paragraphs up? We most certainly had a pattern of grand fights and a flair for drama.

The biggest to note would be the time we broke up. I couldn't tell you the exact reason—I believe it revolved around the amount he was smoking and the fact that I was in my *I am here to fix you into the ideal man when I knew damn well when we met that you were a bad boy* era. This resulted in me placing rules on him (not cool) and him agreeing to them and then lying about it (also not cool). So, in dramatic Gabrielle fashion, I broke up with him. Josh then proceeded to say, "Check mate, bitch," and pulled something even Daniel Day Lewis would tip his hat to.

I got a call from his mother that night that he was being admitted to a seventy-two-hour hold. When I had refused to answer his calls, he had yelled, cried, and threatened to hurt himself. (See, you thought *my* thoughts were crazy? Pubescent boys are *not* to be underestimated.) Those following seventy-two hours I was not allowed to communicate with him. But once he returned home, I received pages and pages of handwritten letters from his time there.

This is one of them.

I can address this to so many nicknames, but the one I truly feel is right is "Angel." I feel you're my angel who looked down on me and lifted this blindfold from my eyes. It really sucks that it took this long and this much pain, but the way I see it...it was one heavy mother-fucking blindfold, and it took one strong-ass girl to lift it. I came here with all the wrong perceptions, looking for "someone" to help me. But the truth is I just had to realize I was strong enough to help myself and find my own ways to lock away my anger and toss the key. Thankfully, I have. I have hurt myself and my loved ones too many times. Without you, kid, I can't say "couldn't" but it would have been much harder. I could never thank you enough. I have finally... in seventeen years...come to peace with myself. I also realized today that another trigger of the anger I had was not made by you leaving me but due to the fact that you deserve much more than I've given you, and I felt it driving me crazy because you weren't happy. You were hurting, and I felt the pain triple because, not only did I lose you, I caused it. A huge chunk of my happiness is caused by how happy you are. And I've realized my world won't end if you won't take me back, as long as you are happy. I love you, girl, and I will do everything in my power to make sure, from this moment on, that you are happy—girlfriend or not. That's your decision, not mine, and I've come to peace with that. I feel such a strong connection with you

*that makes me feel you're my other half, and there's noth-
ing I can do to hide that. But now through all this, I just
know the right way to show you and handle it. I will love
you just as much as that first magical kiss until the day I
die. Thank you. Thank you. Thank you.*

Needless to say, we got back together. This letter not
only proved to me that I could indeed "fix" the men I dated,
but it gave me a sense of pride knowing that I had helped
him find himself in some way. That toxic belief and behavior continued to attract men in my life that I needed (and
felt the responsibility) to fix. It was an endless cycle that
would not be broken until I finally realized my worth—and
that it wasn't tied to fixing people in relationships.

Looking back on this now, it's wild any seven-
teen-year-old can possess these types of feelings and feel as
though they've found their other half so early on. But Josh
was an old soul—and love me until the day he died he did.

The other element of this letter that I find so much
peace in is that he somehow put together what I spent many
years searching for and eventually wrote multiple books
about: *The truth is I just had to realize I was strong enough
to help myself.* What a gift to discover that at seventeen.

By the time he graduated, our relationship was the
longest one either of us had ever had. I went to his prom,
his graduation, and down to San Diego to move him into
college. We did long distance during my senior year, with
the occasional Ross and Rachel *we're on a break* bullshit,
but one thing always remained—our deep love and friendship for each other. He really was my best friend.

I will never, unfortunately, forget the day he left this
earth. I was sound asleep in the condo I was going to be
living in during my first year of college. I had gone out with

friends the night before and had gotten a text from Josh around 1:30 a.m. I will also never forget that text message.

Leaving now. Call you when I get home. Love you.

He never called.

At the time, I assumed he had driven home from the party he was at, which was only ten minutes from his apartment, and had simply forgotten to call before he passed out. So many nights that followed, I wished that was what had taken place.

I woke up to my phone ringing early the next morning. It was a girl from high school that I had been friends with during sophomore year, but we'd had a falling out. It was very strange to see her name pop up on my phone at 7 a.m. I remember groggily answering the phone, which in hindsight was a weird decision in itself. Maybe some part of my subconscious just knew I needed to hear what she had to say.

"Gaby?" Her voice sounded incredibly manic on the other end.

"Yeah?" I waited.

"Josh is dead."

Those of you who have ever experienced a sudden death in your life know there is really no good way of breaking this news to someone. However, if we are going to rank them, this one would be up there as the worst fucking way possible. I didn't even respond. I just hung up the phone. In that moment, I didn't *not* believe her—I was just in too much shock to figure out what the hell to say. Instead, I picked up the phone and called his dad's cell phone. By the time he answered, my shock had begun to transform itself into panic.

"Hello?" I heard his voice.

"Tell me it isn't true." My voice cracked as I waited for an answer. He began to cry on the other end. It was then I started to feel the walls around me closing in. I couldn't understand what had happened—I had just talked to him a few hours earlier. He had just told me he would call me when he got home...

There were three of them in the car that night—Josh, Ryan, and Mike, all who went to our high school. Mike was the only one who survived. When he awoke days later in the hospital with a halo bolted to his head and tubes in his throat, he scribbled Josh's name on a chalkboard with a question mark. When he got the news, he just lay there and cried.

From what we could put together from the news articles and police reports, the boys left the house party around 1:30 a.m. They were all intoxicated and shouldn't have been driving—but everyone at the party insisted that Josh was "more than fine to make it home." As they got off the long freeway offramp, Josh in his BMW and a Toyota pickup truck began to travel at a high speed. Racing? Maybe. Road rage? Who knows. The Toyota clipped the BMW, sending the car out of control and wrapping it around a light pole. Josh and Ryan were declared dead on the scene. The wildest part of all this? A few years earlier, Josh had been driving his truck home in the rain. He skidded out when he hit a slick spot and crashed...*into a light pole*. He walked away that day unscathed, but on August 3rd, 2007, two families lost sons. A sister lost a sibling. A young man lost his brother. And I lost my first love at eighteen.

So many things changed for me that night that it's hard to know where to start unpacking them. For one, the familiar wound of abandonment that my dad's death had left in me was ripped wide open. *When I love someone, they die.*

I mean, seriously, how fucked up is it to lose the first two men your heart chooses to love? If that isn't enough to justify my questionable relationships after that, I don't know what is. Subconsciously, I became so afraid that the men I loved would abandon me, I started to unknowingly attract men who would do just that. How do you think I ended up with a cheating husband or a man that quite literally abandoned me two days before going on a vacation *he* invited me on? If my subconscious was always telling me, "You're going to be abandoned," of course that is going to become my reality—and so it did.

Secondly, it gave me my first real trauma response. From then on, if a boyfriend, family member, or friend ever failed to text or call me when they arrived home after telling me they would, I automatically assumed they were dead. The number of times I created entire scenarios about someone being dead on the side of the road and began to make a game plan of how I would handle my grief and move on with my life would shock you. It's exhausting being inside my head sometimes.

The third, which is a rather dark subject to dive into (what, you mean abandonment and death fantasies don't fall under the comedy section for you?), was that a pattern began which I wouldn't be able to break until my second solo trip more than a decade later. After Josh's death, I *badly* needed to feel safe. To feel connected. To feel wanted. And how does a little girl who lost her daddy feel better? *Attention* from men. How does a barely legal woman who lost her first love feel better? *Desire* from men. And who was there to so graciously hop into bed with me while I grieved and searched for this desire? *Many of his friends.* I'm not proud of this. I contemplated whether I should even write about it. I felt ashamed of it for many years. It wasn't until

I started doing the work on myself and going through my own healing that I realized I had been taken advantage of—and I was able to forgive my eighteen-year-old self for that.

In fact, on my *Eat, Pray, #FML* trip ten years later, I would finally put together the massive belief that began after Josh's death: Sex will keep men close, and therefore I will not be abandoned. It is the one section of the book I get the most messages about. This belief continued to follow me my entire life—attracting men like my ex-husband, who was so sex obsessed that, by the time I left my marriage, I had sexual trauma in my body. Or like the man who broke my heart after my divorce, who I only felt I truly had if we were having sex, resulting in a toxic situationship that completely messed up my definition of what love was. Until I finally discovered this belief and began to consciously make different choices. I chose to not use sex as a tool to keep men close. I finally learned my worth outside of my physical body and began to treat it with the importance it had always deserved. I finally healed the belief that I had to use sex to prevent abandonment, and you know what it brought once I healed it? Tay. A man who would slowly help me undo all the sexual trauma my ex-husband carelessly left in my body. A man who would help redefine my views of what sex and love truly were, because he never made me feel like it was a form of payment or pressure. Through healing that belief, I finally attracted a man who *made me feel safe.*

I am a firm believer, as I will remind you in almost every chapter, that everything happens for a reason. Even when you can't see the *why* when you're in the thick of it all. I'm sure there have been lessons and reasons for everyone who knew Josh. Whether or not the reason was fulfilled depends on whether the person was ready to see it that way and not waste what could be a gift to heal. For me, this experience showed me once again, at an age I was able to comprehend it on a deeper level, how fleeting life is. How strong I am. And most of all, reinforced the abandonment fear that has been my biggest obstacle to overcome thus far in life. I'm proud to say I have healed that (for the most part). Without the loss of my first love reminding me of that subconscious belief, illustrating a clear pattern in my life, I do not know how long it would have taken me to begin that journey. Whenever there is a pattern, it is a clue. Do not ignore them, for they are an invisible map that will guide you to great healing. For me, losing Josh was the moment the map was handed to me—and for that, I say to him, *thank you for the gift you gave me.*

There's something about your first love that you never really forget. Do I think we would have stayed together? Probably not. College years are wild, and we were so young and immature and had so much left to learn. But I do think we would have stayed close. I do think he would have been a dear friend, in my corner, rooting me on as I stumbled and forged my way through life. Alas, what I have now is just that—a guardian angel who has never really left my side.

Who knows why souls choose to leave when they do— but I do believe it is a choice. I've spoken with countless mediums who confirm this, that even when death seems shockingly untimely or unbearably unfair, it is always the *soul's choice.* Usually, the answer is simply that the soul had fulfilled its purpose on earth and could do greater work back home, where we all begin and eventually return to. What magic has Josh been making happen on the other side? What mischief has he been getting into for the past eighteen years? I suspect it's incredible beyond our comprehension if it meant leaving this life with us. I choose to hold onto that. I choose to believe that.

And for those of you who have lost someone in your life and question whether or not there is another side, an afterlife, a heaven—whatever the hell you want to call it—I will leave you with this:

After Josh passed, I was blessed to do a private in-person session with the great John Edward, psychic medium. During the incredible hour, he detailed deeply personal things about Josh to me that *no one* could have known. Toward the end, he said the following words to me:

"He's showing me you driving in a car and there's like...a dozen or so balloons attached to the top of the car. So, as you drive, the balloons are always right above, even though you don't know they're there. He's always going to be with you."

I left the hotel in Beverly Hills that night feeling like I was able to talk to my first love one last time. I stopped and waited at a red light, replaying it all in my head. Just then, across a main intersection, a Jeep drove by with a dozen balloons tied to the top of the ski rack. It all happens for a reason. And I can promise you, we will see them all again.

Taymour

It is no secret amongst all who know me, I'm a sucker for love. Always have been. A hopeless romantic who lives for sappy romance movies and flowers for no reason at all, and there is no doubt where it came from. Let's reflect, shall we? Both my mother and my father were tragic, hopeless romantics. My father, as strong and stoic as he is, is also a huge softy when it comes to romance. He frequently brought home flowers "just because," or stopped dead in his tracks to sweep my mother off her feet and kiss her like they were reenacting the beach scene in *From Here To Eternity*. They were passionate and wildly in love with each other, and it was no secret to anyone. It was glorious to witness at a young age, and it certainly taught me to express those emotions when I had them. They were both Scorpios, one Persian and one Irish. Let that combo sink in for a second. They were madly in love. They were tragic with their love. It was beautiful and scary and wild and magical, and I wanted all of it. As a boy, to be a witness to this roller coaster... my goodness. As it turns out, what I thought was wild and beautiful and magical...was actually a dysfunctional and toxic representation of love.

For as long as my memory serves me, I have been searching for "The One." It was a running joke amongst my friends growing up. I would fall in love and go confidently shouting to my friends, "GUYS, THIS IS THE ONE!" or "SHE'S THE ONE!" or "I'm *REALLY* sure she's the one this time!" I mean, I probably said it every different way, one thousand times. I almost didn't even need to say it before I got the response, "Let us guess..."

I'm not sure what it was for me, but there was an intense draw to find that love of my life. Looking back, therein lay the reason I became the serial monogamist that I am. We could probably go through each of these chapters and find a through line of my actions relating back to my mother's death. Listen, folks, it ain't a secret—trauma can be like a wrecking ball. Only Miley Cyrus isn't swinging around on it naked. It sucks. Safe to say that it applies to this chapter as well. Let me explain.

My mother passed when I was thirteen—which left an undeniable void in my existence. It left me yearning for that affection. So even though I was already into girls in a pretty big way, I was about to enter high school and the pond was about to get a lot bigger. I went batshit crazy my freshman and sophomore years. I think I had six girlfriends those two years, all of whom were most definitely *the one*. None of them lasted for more than a few months. There was Sarah, there was Kim, there was Jen. There was Vanessa and Joanna and Kara. I mean, really. All of those relationships occurred in the five to ten months after my mom suddenly died. Sheesh. If that isn't a serious sign of abandonment damage, I don't know what is.

Once I got to college, the relationships became more serious, and I started having substantial feelings other than just replacement and pleasure. There was comfort and blossoming love that I could not ignore. They were solid, and they were bringing out the romantic in me. I wanted that crazy passionate love I'd witnessed my parents have and was gonna stop at nothing until I got it. And so began my search for the highs and lows, the scary and poetic, the passion that my parents showed me—even though it was unhealthy. It was everything I wanted. And let me tell you that when you are searching high and wide for something that you want THAT badly, and you think you've found it, you don't ever want to let it go. We all have that first love and we all have that first heartbreak. They are not always the same, but when they are it's all the more difficult.

Being the serial monogamist that I am, I would go from relationship to relationship in search of *the one*. I would fall in love hard and quickly and then pull back. Or sometimes they would pull back. But in the end, I'd realize that it just wasn't the right match. I would pop in and out of relationships that would not last more than six months. I did manage to remain in a relationship during my college years that lasted about a year, which was new territory for me, but looking back I can assuredly say that I was not *in love,* rather just comfortable with the monotony. Incidentally, she ended up cheating on me, which not only ended that relationship but opened up a lot of wounds related to abandonment. In hindsight, I wasn't mature enough for love at that point in my life and was clearly just trying to fill the void left by my mother's passing. I needed to live some more. I needed to NOT go looking for *the one.* I just needed to focus on myself and what I wanted to do with the rest of my life. So I started to do that. And the moment I started to love myself and care for myself was the very moment I fell in love. Funny how that works.

Her name was Amy. I was madly in love with her, and she broke my heart into a million little pieces. Yuck, that sounds like a lyric to a crappy teen love song. When Amy came into my life, it was the right match...or so I thought. A little history. My father and her father were childhood friends which, of course, added fodder to the flame. We had known each other our whole lives and to me that was what had been missing in all my prior relationships. Not so much the actual history between us but the connection or bond that we already shared. And now we were both willing to take the relationship to another level as adults. It was super romantic to me. There was something tangible that we had in common. It was comforting but was also the one ingredient that made it special and magical. Until then, I had been unaware of how deep my love could go because—WHOA—I was falling and falling hard.

Although we initially kept the relationship a secret, in fear our families would be against it, we eventually started to settle in nicely to our future. God, you gotta love that honeymoon phase. We moved in together and spent a lot of quality time with both families. It truly was an amazing period of our lives. We were coming up to the two-year mark, and I had never felt like that before, nor did I think it could get better. I hadn't gotten as far as looking for rings, but I was definitely getting close to pulling the trigger. Then one night, at my cousin's wedding, everything changed...and it all started with an innocent little conversation.

As we enjoyed being guests at the wedding, marriage had begun to flutter around my little brain at every turn. I decided it was the perfect time to casually go for a walk and bring it up. Now, I don't know if it was a certain vibe I was putting out, but I think she panicked and thought I was just going to drop down on a knee right there. Needless to say, I didn't drop down on a knee, nor was I planning to, I was just gauging where she was at with it. You know, just dipping my toes in to see if the water was warm. Well, the water was not warm. It was bitterly cold. I'm sure she could sense where I was aiming to go in the relationship, and she was absolutely *not* ready for that. She was a few years younger than me and fresh out of college. I mean, really, who is ready for that kind of relationship in their twenties? I apparently wasn't even ready for that type of relationship in my thirties...or a portion of my forties.

About a month or so after that night at my cousin's wedding, she broke up with me. To say that it devastated me would be a gross understatement. I wish someone had warned me that the first love is always the hardest to overcome. I was not ready for the pain and certainly didn't have the tools to deal with that heartbreak. To this day, I still remember that hurt very well. I painstakingly trudged through each step of the grieving process as if my life depended on it and, in some ways, it did.

I sometimes make my life a little harder than it needs to be. I began making some unhealthy life choices, which you will assuredly read about in the addiction chapter, and my family began to worry about me. Up until that point, even with my mother's death, my family always saw me full of life and vibrance—of which, I suddenly had none. I just couldn't imagine life without her. Everything was so perfect, or so I thought. But there I was, not having to *imagine* life without her. I was actually *experiencing* it. And it sucked. It was a wicked tailspin that I couldn't pull out of.

Little did I know I was being introduced to one of my major life tasks—*to learn how to be okay being alone.* My grief for the loss of my girlfriend was magnified by the fact that I had developed serious abandonment issues at an early age. I was a serial monogamist for a reason. I hated being alone because it reminded me of the void my mother had left. I was living with the core belief that I needed to have a replacement for my mom, who abandoned me, and I continued living with it for another fifteen years. I wish I had been insightful enough to realize the connection between *being okay to be alone* and that insatiable need to find *the one*. It is all pretty textbook. I just couldn't bear the thought of being alone, so I deemed everyone *the one,* until they weren't. It was an obvious pattern that I established for myself in response to losing my mom. I just couldn't see it. And now, with the pain of a broken heart, I wasn't about to start looking for answers. I just wallowed in my pain for a good six to eight months and refused to look within for what I needed. Instead, I looked outside of myself. I needed a change in scenery, a new beginning, a new spark.

So, after what felt like an eternity of dark times, I did what any grief-stricken, broken-hearted thirty-something would do. *I went to Europe.* Yup, just like Gabrielle in *Eat, Pray, #FML*, I went to Europe to get over a broken heart. Although our stories are vastly different, there are many similarities. The absolutely wild parties that never ended, the precarious encounters you'd rather forget. I was youngish, hungry, pretending to be happy, and absolutely ready for anything. And honestly, anything and everything was had. Like Gabs, the experience was life-changing in so many ways, but unlike her, I didn't write a book about it. Oh, the stories I could tell.

I set out on a journey to get over a broken heart, but at every turn I thought of Amy. I thought it was going to be easy, especially in Europe. But it wasn't. I occupied my mind with writing as much as I could. I have always been big on keeping journals and what a better time and place to pour out your feelings on paper. I would write by day and party by night. My buddy who was traveling with me was newly single as well, which made the trip more female focused, but we both set out to heal whatever it was that needed healing. Didn't someone say one time that the best way to heal a broken heart is to *jump in the sack* with someone else? If they did, it was terrible fucking advice. While there is a time and a place for it, getting your mind off the past in this way is simply a Band-Aid. The gaping wound still lies bleeding underneath.

When you're cruising around Europe single in your early thirties, look out. On our first night in Madrid, I stood on our balcony overlooking the Rio Manzanares and thought to myself, *Tonight is the night.* There is always that first person you hook up with after a significant breakup that sets the tone for the rest of your mourning. With the rain approaching the city and the heat rising, there was a certain humidity that turned me and the whole city electric. My buddy and I got ready for a night on the town. We shared a bottle of wine to watch the sun go down from our balcony and planned a nice dinner, followed by a flamenco show because, you know, when in Madrid. We walked the cobblestone streets on the way to the restaurant with a certain gauche confidence. I don't know what it is about me, but when I want something and put my mind to it, it's probably going to happen. That night, I was going to meet a girl. That is all. I wasn't setting out to have sex or anything more than just meeting someone cool. I wanted to be interested in someone else for a change. To find beauty in someone at face value. So yeah, I had a certain strut in my step, the same strut I've had the nights many of my relationships began. But most importantly, I wasn't thinking about Amy.

Approaching our quaint little Spanish restaurant, we passed a dozen or so two-tops nestled nicely on the cobblestone. Most of the tables were taken, and I made eye contact with two girls dining together. Confidently and without warning, I pulled a chair up to their table and said apologetically, "I am so sorry we're late." My friend was completely caught off guard, as were the two women sitting there enjoying their meal. To be totally honest, as confident as I am, I surprised even myself that night. It was one of those spur-of-the-moment decisions that I didn't think through. I just sprang into action and planned on improvising my way through it. Sometimes it works and sometimes you fall flat on your face. This could've gone either way.

As soon as the immediate confusion subsided and they realized this was just a silly ruse, one of the girls cleverly winked at me and followed with, "Well...we didn't know if you'd make it, so we started without you." Oh shit, this girl was better at this than me. This was gonna be fun. Turned out they were Americans doing the same thing we were doing—mending broken hearts and/or sowing their oats, both of which required quite a bit of fun to be had, and quite a bit of sangria to be drunk. There was something about this girl's energy that had me twisted. She was gorgeous but also had a devious side that she was not about to hide. Within two minutes of us sitting at the table, she and I were holding hands—and her hands apparently wanted to roam. It was like she was the female version of me, going through exactly what I was going through, and our worlds happened to collide on this night to fix what was once broken. We sat there for about an hour, laughing and talking about our lives. I wanted to kiss her so badly, I almost leaned in there at the table, but I'm glad I didn't. There is something to be said about your first kiss with someone. It's meaningful regardless of who it's with. We finished up dinner and decided to go to the flamenco show together, in hopes they would be able to fit us in. Just as we arrived, the Spanish rain came through. It felt musky and hot, and everyone was on the verge of sweat. After the flamenco performance, we danced and enjoyed a few more cocktails.

While the rain poured down, we decided to make a run for it to the next spot. Bad choices sometimes lead to romantic interludes. The rain was too heavy, so we had to duck into an overhang that barely covered the two of us. At that point, it didn't matter—we were absolutely drenched. We were huddled in, trying our best to stay out of the rain, when we caught each other's eyes. It was straight out of a movie. Both of my hands up and around her face, the rain streaming down both of our cheeks. It was a wildly spectacular kiss. Neither one of us wanted it to end. It was sheer romance, and we were all caught up in it. The kiss that shook my soul did eventually end but certainly left its mark. The rain was too intense for us to do anything further that night and then the weirdest yet most beautiful thing happened. We looked at each other and just as I was about to ask for her information, she stopped me and said something profound.

"Let's just not. Let's just have tonight and never forget what happened here in the rain."

It almost brought a tear to my eye. Not because I wanted more but because it was so fucking perfect. End it as if it actually were a movie. I couldn't have suggested something better, and there she went into a taxi, leaving me standing in the rain. It was one of those experiences that you never forget—and it was the first time I hadn't thought about my ex since my heart had broken. Baby steps.

Those baby steps started to turn into adult steps and soon enough I was running. The rest of my trip had a few more encounters like this but none so monumental. I continued my writing and continued to heal my wounds until I was finally ready to come back and resume my life. Upon my return, I felt rejuvenated and was finally seeing the light at the end of the tunnel. I was able to move past it all and just at the perfect time. Amy began dating someone and if I hadn't been mentally prepared for that, it would have most definitely sent me into another tailspin. But no—I was organically moving on and it felt right. Life just kept moving, and I decided not to stay in that place anymore. I guess that was one of the lessons: *Grieve for however long it takes to move past it without pushing it down.* Well, that and kiss the random girl in the fucking rain.

It just so happens, Amy and I have remained family friends and will continue to do so. We don't see each other regularly, but I always want the very best for her and her wonderful family. She has an amazing husband and beautiful children, and they will always have a special place in my heart. She unintentionally taught me a great many lessons about myself that I would otherwise not have been given. And here, after this first heartbreak, was where I started to uncover that deep core belief the abandonment left that I would need to come to terms with: *I am not enough.* I am not enough without a partner, without love, without a job, without something other than just...*myself.* This was one of the life-altering events that made me reevaluate the way I thought about myself. The heartbreak forced me to figure out why I felt so lost without her—but more importantly it made me connect the dots between the abandonment I felt and this notion of not being enough. The love I felt from my mother always blanketed me with warmth, and now that it was gone, life felt cold and I could not find the warmth I yearned for. I was not content alone and that needed to change. I realized that I couldn't just move from relationship to relationship, searching for that warmth. I needed to be able to warm myself. But as anyone who has been on an epic healing journey can tell you, before you can see the light at the end of the tunnel, you have to make your way through a sometimes dark and terrifying cave—and my journey would take me down to depths I was not prepared to go.

Addiction

"You are not weak for struggling.
You are strong for continuing to fight."
– Anonymous

Gabrielle

Addiction can come in many forms, with faces you run from in nightmares and depths you can only feel when you've sunk far below rock bottom. While Tay will paint a picture of where most people's brains go when they hear the word "addiction," I'll be taking you down a road less often traveled but dark and deadly in different ways. What road, you ask? It's a long, winding path into the gray and dreary valley of eating disorders, with jagged rocks of body dysmorphia and claw-like branches tearing at your flesh, which society has deemed "fat." It's a path that for a long time I have tried to step off and erase the tracks to. A path I have, for years, pretended wasn't a real problem when I knew damn well it was. A path I have never openly taken people down...until now.

I can tell you the exact moment my eating disorder began. Perhaps the LA lifestyle, middle school pressures, and time spent in one of the most vain industries there is—Hollywood—laid the groundwork. But the moment the thoughts became a problem? There was no mistaking that.

I guess this is the point I'm supposed to give a trigger warning for what's to come? Although isn't that true for literally this entire book? However, this chapter specifically will have some dark thoughts and graphic details—ones I'm happy no longer plague me.

I grew up a dancer. I loved to dance. The freedom in my body. The emotional expression. And I was *good*. I loved the dance studio I was trained at. I ended up teaching there for years once I graduated, and I still consider the owner to be family. It wasn't a competition studio—it was a studio that nurtured passion.

When I was in eighth grade, my mom threw her annual Christmas party, and one of my teachers from the studio came. She was younger, in her early thirties, and very edgy. Her choreography was so different. I loved her classes. As I was stuffing my face with some typical holiday treat, she looked over at me, and said, "You better be careful how much you're eating, or you won't be jumping very high, woman!" She laughed, not thinking much of it, I'm sure. My twelve-year-old brain sat up in my head and promptly decided that I needed to rectify the situation—because who was I if I was not one of the best in the class, able to fly and jump across the stage? The subconscious message in that? Who was I if I was not *skinny*?

All eating disorders are different, and people experience and identify with them in a very unique and personal way. So I won't sit here and pretend I know a ton about the subject or all the ins and outs of a specific one. But I can tell you what it looked like for me.

I was never a candidate for anorexia. I'm a foodie to this day and always have been. There were times I would try to not eat for a day, and it was most definitely not for me. What I was a candidate for? Bulimia. God, I hate even typing the word out. What a gross disease—eating whatever you want and then shoving your fingers down your throat to bring it all back up. For what? The vanity of fitting into a pair of jeans or looking good in a bikini? What's so dangerous about this disease is that (for me, at least) it begins to become less about the weight and more about the control. And if there is any through line in my life, it's *control*, even to this day. I love having control. I love being in control. Why? Because when I'm in control, Daddy doesn't die. When I'm in control, Josh doesn't get killed. When I'm in control, people don't cheat, I'm not heartbroken, and everything can go to plan. So naturally, whenever I felt like I was losing control in my life, I desperately searched for what I *could* control, and that was what was going into—and coming out of—my body.

When it first started in high school, I wasn't very good at it. I vividly remember being in my teenage bedroom after my grandmother died and heading into the bathroom to throw up an apple. *An apple.* A maximum of one hundred calories with nutrient value. But it wasn't about the calories or the weight those calories (wouldn't) put on. It was about being able to decide I was going to do something and then execute it. I didn't have control over Nana dying and the triggers it brought up in me—but I sure had control over seeing that apple in the toilet.

Then I actually learned how to do it.

I first read the book *The Best Little Girl in the World* in high school. It's a coming-of-age novel about a fictional character who struggles with an eating disorder. It has since been adapted into a TV movie and won the American Library Association Best Book for Young Adults Award. You know what else it did? Taught me how to have an eating disorder. That's not knocking the book or its subject matter, by any means. If an individual is going to fall into any type of addiction, there's something inside of them (I believe) that is meant to go through that situation in order to learn the lessons or heal something in this life. I guess what I'm getting at is that I would have found my way into the disease whether I read it in a book, saw it on television, or heard about it at school. I think this book was actually intended to show you the dark side of it and scare people away from it—the tagline on the cover is *"The bestselling novel about the obsession that kills"*—but for me it did the opposite.

Over two decades later, I only remember one part from the book. The main character, Kessie, is mainly dealing with anorexia, but there is one chapter where she discovers that if her parents are going to force her to eat, she can simply throw it up. I learned a few things from this section. One, that you can throw up what you eat, and it would essentially cancel out the calories you consumed. Two, if you eat ice cream after said food, it will come up a lot easier. And three, you have to hide the evidence. The book spoke about a ring that will begin to develop inside the toilet bowl from the bacteria of the food, and that often, when throwing up, the force of the muscles contracting will sometimes cause you to urinate. I have many memories of my eating disorder but none quite as shameful as soaking up puddles of piss from the bathroom floor after purging.

As I'm sure Tay will share with you, no one is a better liar than someone hiding an addiction. An actor with an addiction? You do not stand a chance. *I choose* not to lie to people in my life because I love them, and your integrity and your word is quite literally all you have at the end of the day. But when I *choose* to lie? Trust me—you will never know it. And that is terrifying.

I remember times when a boyfriend would question me if I had been lazy about cleaning the toilet or when they noticed other signs. This is when I came up with a new tactic. Admission. Not to something being wrong, but to the act of throwing up.

"I have a really bad stomachache. I'm gonna see if I can throw up to feel better." Or "I don't feel good, I'm gonna go to the bathroom." Maybe they were just dumb or maybe they just didn't care but, either way, I always got away with it. It's a fucked-up talent when you can go to the bathroom, throw up everything you ate, and be back at the table in under five minutes. Most of the time, no one will question you.

I want to be clear, there were times I would go months and months without throwing up and not even think about it. My eating disorder wasn't always rearing its disgusting head for the world to see. It would ebb and flow. More often than not, it was sitting silently, just a few layers beneath the surface, waiting for the vulnerability to hit my brain. Then it would tap me gently on the shoulder, whisper in my ear, and remind me that I did in fact have control over something.

The random flare-ups lasted on and off even through my first marriage. As talented as my ex-husband thought he was with his lies and deception, imagine living with someone for five years, sharing a home and a bathroom quite intimately, and having zero idea that your partner (at times) had a full-blown eating disorder. It only took me one afternoon to find the evidence of his cheating. He never knew more about my eating disorder than what I chose to tell him.

My addiction came out more frequently during my first marriage, partly because on some subconscious level I felt so out of control in that relationship and never truly safe, and partly because my ex-husband would continuously make comments about my body. Whether or not I was looking "up to par," or what trainer I should see. For all intents and purposes, he encouraged a super unhealthy body dysmorphia. I recently saw a photo my cousin posted from the night before my first wedding. It's a simple photo of us hugging and my hand is grasping her arm as we hug. It doesn't look like the hand of a woman about to get married the next day—it looks like a skeleton grasping onto a life raft before she's tossed out to sea. The most disturbing part of it all? My soon-to-be husband was consistently telling me how amazing I looked and perpetuating me losing more and more weight. The photos from my first wedding and during that time period? I look sick. Sure, bulimia had taken a backseat and extreme diet and overexercise were currently driving the car, but nevertheless, I was sick. But when your husband has a specific image of the body of a nineteen-year-old blonde in his mind, of course he's going to say skip the fries and hit the gym...*again*. And you know, dye your hair blonder while you're at it.

There were nights over the years I would make the conscious decision to have a binge and purge night. I would watch a show, order or buy whatever food I wanted, eat and watch TV, and go throw it all up when I needed to. Sometimes this cycle would repeat multiple times that night. Was there shame? Of course. Did I know it was unhealthy? Obviously. Did it matter? Not in the slightest. *It's not like I'm doing it all the time*, I would rationalize it in my head. *It's fine. I'm in control.*

After my divorce and the heartbreak that happened immediately after, I was so incredibly broken down and insecure about...everything. I had never felt more out of control my entire life, but I knew I wanted to be healthy. I desperately tried to stuff the toxic inner dialogue down. And what was left in place of that? Hyper-focus on my body.

There's not much I regret about what is written in *Eat, Pray, #FML*, but there are two things I wish I would have included. One, the fact that I sold my wedding ring to pay for the month-long European trip, and that the entire adventure cost roughly $5,000. The other is the deep pain I was in as I struggled with my body dysmorphia and eating disorder. After the book became popular, I got a handful of comments online that I was fat shaming and fatphobic because I kept harping on myself for eating too much and gaining weight. It's very true, I was hyper-aware of all of it— but not because I care what size people are or think there's anything wrong with different body shapes. I actually think that's incredibly beautiful. It was simply because I had kept myself in eating purgatory for so many years and, instead of authentically writing about it all, that is how it ended up coming out.

I didn't throw up on that trip (other than from a night of too much alcohol), and it was wildly difficult for me because I did eat, a lot. Now add in the man who broke my heart making comments on the weight that I'd gained and a new thyroid issue from all the stress I was dealing with, which kept that weight on. I no longer had my control. Welcome to the worst depression I had ever fallen into.

That trip changed me in so many ways. I uncovered deep subconscious beliefs that had been driving my adult life for years. I learned how to be alone—and most importantly, how to be okay with that. And, finally, I learned to love myself. Loving yourself isn't as easy as people make it seem. Until quite recently, after becoming a mother, I had never been able to look in the mirror and say "I love you, Gabrielle. You're beautiful." I felt like a crazy person. Until I learned that loving myself was as simple as doing things that make my soul feel and experience love. Something that fell under that new way of living? Taking care of my physical body. I made a commitment to myself at the end of 2019, after I came back from my second solo trip, that I would never make myself throw up ever again. By this time, it was happening very rarely. I told Tay about my commitment. I had shared my past struggles with him, but I don't think anyone in my life knew that it was still a cancer living deep inside, waiting to be called upon when I needed to feel control. I went all of 2020 without purging, which, considering how many days we indulged in Postmates during the pandemic, is fucking impressive, even to me. Then one day, on a day not even important enough for me to remember the details of it, I made myself throw up. Only this time, I went to Tay and told him.

You will always hear from addiction specialists that part of recovery is relapse. That is true for any form of addiction. It only took that one slip up, and the deep pain I felt from letting myself down, to make me know that I was done. So done, that during my pregnancy, when I experienced nausea that probably would have been helped by throwing up, I wouldn't allow my fingers anywhere near my mouth to assist in that process.

The last real trigger that came up for me was reading Jennette McCurdy's book, *I'm Glad My Mom Died*. At one point while she's struggling with a horrific eating disorder, she writes about being in the early stages of recovery—and how doctors don't classify you as having an eating disorder unless you're throwing up at least once a week for three months. So...does that mean I didn't "technically" ever have a *recognized* eating disorder? How weird of a scale is that to judge what has so clearly been an unhealthy habit in my life for so long. It almost felt like the diagnostic criteria was saying, "It's okay if you do it every once and a while. Nothing to beat yourself up about."

The other thing that book gave me was the very important reminder to not let a slip become a slide. So often, especially with control issues, once we cross the threshold, we quickly allow ourselves to spiral downward into the depths of the dark. Instead, now, I give myself grace. I don't need to wait to start eating better on a Monday. I don't need to start saving money at the beginning of a new month. I don't need to wait for New Year's to make resolutions. I can make mistakes and rectify them in that moment. I don't need to dive headfirst into the spiral.

That lesson has served me in all areas of my life. Not to allow something small to become something bigger than it needs to be. Not to allow a fight to ruin a trip—or a disappointment to ruin a relationship. The moment you can look at the negatives in your life as a detective, trying to find the lessons or the value in them, they cease to really be negatives at all. Instead, they become opportunities for growth, lessons of wisdom, and invaluable moments of change.

Never in a million years would I have been open with one of my past partners about the depths of my eating disorder. Nor would I have invited them to help me hold myself accountable. It was only because I had learned to love myself and see myself in a new way that I was able to finally invite Tay into that part of my past. Our relationship has only been strengthened by that. The idea of that used to terrify me—because *what if they take away my control*? Turns out, being open with Tay and having a safe place where someone will hold space for me and allow my missteps has allowed me to *breathe*. To continue to let go of the need for control. Don't we beat ourselves up enough to begin with? Why on earth would you want a partner who is going to do more of that for you?

Healing my addiction to control my food—or the control the food had over me—has given me a sense of power. It has shown me that I truly have the authority to change anything in my life if I want it badly enough. The world sometimes lies and tells us that there are things beyond our control. That addiction is a disease and there is nothing you can do about it. In my life, I choose not to believe that. I choose to know that I have control over my thoughts, my actions, and myself. And that has given me my power back. Being able to fully let go of my control issues? Well...that's a work in progress.

I'm happy to report that I've written this chapter in one sitting, while eating an egg sandwich with cheese on thick sourdough toast, without a second thought about the calories or their effect. After the birth of my son, I feel so differently toward my body. I was worried that I would panic about the way my figure looked or how my body had changed. But truly, I'm just thankful. Thankful that my body was able to carry him, thankful that I've fed him with the nutrients my body made, and thankful that I finally feel relaxed in my own skin. And when that little toxic voice taps me on the shoulder and attempts to whisper in my ear now, I kindly tell it to shut the fuck up. I no longer have any room for it in my life—and feeling that? It's absolute freedom.

Taymour

This is going to be hard. Not for the reasons you may think. Not because I don't want to relive the experiences—because as I mentioned earlier, my experiences are my history, my DNA. I try to regret very little. What worries me with this chapter is my children reading it. There, I said it. It's a huge step for me to do this. You see, during my addiction days, I wrote countless journals of despair and self-loathing, self-destruction and resilience, and how those two words were a thriving and breathing war inside of me for a long time. Although those journals are not being published, I do wonder what my kids will think when they eventually read this. Thankfully, neither of them will be reading this anytime soon. My oldest is just starting to enjoy chapter books, and my youngest is currently having a love affair with Ms. Rachel—I have time. It isn't that I am ashamed of the path I took to get here. It is that, to my children, I am extremely influential, and I don't want them to emulate that path in any way. So, yeah, this is hard. I will tread lightly while staying completely true. But make no mistake, one day I will sit down with them and truly express my path, my wrongdoings, and the dangers they presented for me. Today is not that day. Today, I write to you, my trusted readers, and I write to myself. I write to acknowledge where I was and stand strong and tall when I look at where I am now—because it was not an easy journey to get here.

Pretty sure every addiction counselor on the face of the planet would link addiction to past trauma. Not necessarily past-life trauma, just trauma that has occurred in your life at one point or another. It wasn't much different for me. The loss of my mother left me alone, angry, and wistful. But those feelings were not at the surface. They were deep inside. I actually came across as very put-together in my first year of high school, which was some four months after my mom died. Those feelings were certainly not addressed. Look, there's no secret recipe. When you have feelings, it is best to process them then and there. When you bury them, push them aside, or compartmentalize them, they don't go away...they come back with a vengeance. It isn't a myth. It's factual science and it is related to the nervous system. We push these feelings down, and they grow into something unmanageable. And for what? Because we didn't want to sit in the emotion right when it was happening? Or go to therapy and discuss proper ways of handling such life-altering events, like the death of a parent? At the time, I just didn't possess the tools to deal with such a thing. That was glaringly obvious. Needless to say, my emotions festered deep within, and came back to bite me in the ass.

I'm not gonna lie or try to sugarcoat this is any way. I love to party and always have. I love being social and I love a great shindig. I love the potential these get-togethers present to make things go wild and, for me, wild was always right around the corner. I used to be the first one at the party and ALWAYS the last to leave—usually the next day. I was the life of the party, which itself stemmed from something deeper than I could see at the time. I was filling voids left and right, but dammit, was I having fucking fun doing it. I always had the drugs on me. and I was always the loudest in the room. I was on fire back then. Electric. I felt like Jim Carey in *The Mask*, when he was wearing the infamous green disguise. Unstoppable and enigmatic, I barreled through those early days never considering the proverbial mask would eventually be pulled off. But I have to admit that as crazy and wild as some of those times were, I regret very little. I guess looking back I wish I had just a touch more vision about why I had the need to take things to such extremes.

I've always been one to experiment and when in college experimenting was the weekend norm. It was cocaine one weekend, followed by acid the next, and some mushrooms and ecstasy to round out the month. Welcome to the nineties. I went to school at the University of Oregon, a mecca for wild partying and even wilder psychedelics. Being out on my own for the first time brought a new sense of freedom, and I didn't recognize a problem. I chalked it up to being a typical college student and partying with the rest of 'em. I was also a fairly good student and stayed focused on studying, if you can believe it. It wasn't until a year or so after college that I became aware that there were times when I couldn't stop.

Once out of school, the *using* started with cocaine—copious amounts of it. I was living in San Francisco at the time, and it was everywhere. Cocaine and ecstasy were all the rage, and I was all up in it. I could no longer chalk it up to having fun in college. I was no longer in college anymore and, like most overindulgences, was no longer having fun.

Addiction in my life came in waves. Three to be exact. The first was during my mid-twenties. The second was during my late twenties to early thirties. And the third during my early forties. These waves lasted roughly two years each. They were all severe and potentially fatal had I not pulled out at the exact moments that I did. It is very scary to look back at your life and not have enough fingers or toes to count how many times you should've died.

The first of these waves was more experimental and somewhat controlled. There was definitely a problem, but it was more like floating in the wave pool before the machine turns on to wreak havoc on your little inner tube and thrash you around like a fucking ragdoll. This was the calmest of the three.

I was in my mid-twenties, managing our family bar and basically living on Jack Daniels, cocaine, and Marlboro reds. Heavier drugs made their way into my world here and there, but they were just glimpses of what was to come. What got me out of that first wave was a change of location and direction in life. I had just started acting in San Francisco and was starting to pick up some steam, and the obvious move was to Los Angeles. I booked my first film, which was to be shot in Los Angeles and Mexico, and I was off and running. The passion of my creativity in acting superseded my desire to be high, and that first wave began to naturally die down—or did it?

Looking back, I realize that that first wave needed to be addressed diligently, not just run from. But run I did. So, although I didn't face the storm of that first wave head on, I did escape it. After shooting the movie, I settled in nicely to the Hollywood lifestyle. Sure, I was partying with the rest of Los Angeles, but it was more controlled, as I was focused on booking my next film and building the creative path of my future. This first wave lasted two years, and thankfully I came out of it unscathed and motivated. Until the second wave approached without warning.

I had been down in Los Angeles for about three years, and the acting thing wasn't hitting like I planned. It was time to get an actual paying job, so I did what most other out-of-work actors in Los Angeles do—went back to bartending. I never thought of alcohol being a trigger or gateway for me in the beginning, but looking back I can safely say that it was. It was the chivalrous knight in shining armor to my demon, opening the door and letting him through. The late-night drinking quickly turned into early morning partying and, before I knew it, I was swept away.

I often look back and wonder how the majority of my friends that partied back then were able to control it. Those countless urges that lurked behind every corner just to stay up a little bit later. The inability to even go to bed if there was more in your pocket. I didn't understand how people could just dip their toe in and not want to do a big fucking cannonball.

I guess they weren't addicts.

I am.

There I was, starting to feel some of the same feelings I felt in San Francisco, that desperate fire of not wanting to stop, the utter helplessness of not being able to stop. Night in and night out, after all the rowdy fun had subsided, after everyone else was asleep, there I stood on the precipice of a cavernous void with the earth below me beginning to shift and give way. I knew where it was going, yet I was too weak to make a change, so again I turned a blind eye with a savage mentality of having the most fun possible...and sweeping away any feelings of discomfort or grief.

Welcome to wave two.

This wave wasn't as easy as the previous one. This one hurt and did some damage. Unfortunately, I got into heavier substances than cocaine. Cocaine became boring and monotonous, and I was constantly in search of more, more, more. I needed something different. I am an upper type of addict. I don't like downers. So heroin was never my thing. Nor were any type of pills. If they had been my thing, I probably wouldn't be here to tell you about it. No, I was going the other direction. Speed, baby. Let's go faster. Give this ride some fucking gas and let's take off. Speed in any form. You name it, I was looking for it. I cringe when I say it, but those are the facts. I lived in a pocket of Venice Beach where whatever I was craving was being sold right outside my door. It took me to places I never want to be. EVER AGAIN. If there are any readers out there who know what that feels like and got out of it, then pause and salute yourself. It is a devastating low that holds you down like barbed wire—any time you attempt to escape, it tightens its grasp.

I did in fact get out of that episode with a change of living location, but for the second time, I didn't address *why* I was doing this. I was escaping something...numbing something. But what? I felt I was old enough to have processed my mother's death by this point, so I didn't look into that, which was an obvious mistake. I didn't look into anything, for that matter, because I wasn't prepared to see what I might find. I spoke to a few therapists, but they were all short-lived. Any time the therapist would try to enter past my superficial shell, I would run. Classic story. So it was a change of location and another chance for me to bury it all deeper.

Fast-forward ten years and there I was, lying face up in a turbulent ocean, with waves getting bigger and bigger. A lifetime had happened in the previous ten years. I got married. We had a child. I got divorced. And just as my ex-wife and I were going through our separation, I saw this massive rogue wave approaching, and it could not be stopped. In my every breath I felt it: *This wave was gonna kill my hopes and dreams—and maybe even me.*

This was the angry kind, the violent kind. The kind that does damage to your body, soul, and spirit. The kind your family cannot recover from, regardless of whether you live or die. This was the bottom of the barrel, and I stand here to tell you that when you're addicted to drugs, or anything for that matter, there is no redemption until you've found yourself in a fetal position at the bottom of that dark, cold barrel. I started thinking that the only way to escape was to go further down and hold onto the hope that my body had the resilience to get me out of it—this one last time.

My ex-wife and I were splitting child care duties at first, but as the wave took over me, it became clear that I was in trouble, and soon my ability to care for my daughter became questionable. As *heart wrenching* as that is to write, it was my unfortunate truth at the time. I had started working at a different nightclub in Hollywood. You can see where this is going. The shift started at 10 p.m. and I would usually get home around 5 a.m. This place was wild. It was a machine and was my recipe for disaster.

My ex and daughter had moved out, and there was no one to answer to. The late-night bartending shifts became the excuse I needed to get me *through* the...well...late nights. Lo and behold, just outside my front door in Hollywood a guy was selling *something.* I bought it, and just like that, I was caught up in a wave that lasted almost three years. *Three years*. What a wild amount of time to just toss away.

It happens like that for an addict. That is why people say, "Once an addict, always an addict." The beast is in there, make no mistake about it. It just comes down to the control you have over it. I do believe in reform and second chances and know personally about resilience, so I don't always agree with the above statement. For me, there are things that I will never, EVER do again. Ever. I will have a drink here or there, and I use my fair share of marijuana. But I have diligently remained away from coke or anything stronger. The takeaway? Every person is different and to each their own.

Once I was well down the spiral, that ever-so-faint realization that I'd had going into this one started rearing its disfigured head. I knew that I had to deal with this in a different way. There was no escaping this monster like the last two waves. So many people go through addiction just trying to find a way out when the way out requires looking further in. Addiction comes from inside of you, but I couldn't look in. Not yet. I ended up entering an outpatient Buddhist rehab for forty-five days. All the while, my ex-wife, God bless her, still allowed me to see my daughter.

Once that was complete, life started to get better. I did have my relapses here and there. I did make mistakes, which is what addicts do. But I regularly went to NA meetings for close to a year. I attempted to take the steps. But it wasn't any program or philosophy or even the possibility of losing my child that pulled me out of it. It was me and me alone. All of the answers were inside of me—*so I finally began looking in.*

I had not yet processed the grief I still held onto surrounding my mother's death, so I began analyzing that. I went to therapy. I sought help. I was finally truthful with myself, and everyone involved. It was only once I started to face the grief with the help of therapy and my wonderful aunt, Mama Goose, a psychologist and substance-abuse specialist, that I was able to acknowledge the *reason* I was numbing.

Then an odd thing happened. Once I came face-to-face with all of my suffering and really started to process the loss of my mother, I began to feel comfortable within myself. I could feel a little shift in the way I looked at myself. It felt like I was getting some of my power back. Really, it was an easy concept to understand. You see, my mother, even when we fought, showered me with such positive attention it was like I was constantly standing in the sun. And then one day, that sun was no longer shining, and I was left in the darkness. I yearned for it. So I went to find it elsewhere. I was fun and infectious when I was using and, for a fleeting moment, I felt as if I was back in her warm rays. But it wasn't real—and with every comedown, I was met with more darkness.

Finally, my wave rescinded, and I was left with a new sense of purpose. I wasn't going back down that road again. I was done with feeling that way. Done with letting people down...mainly myself. Done with not living up to my full potential. Just done. Thankfully, I had people who never left my corner during all of it. My amazing aunt and my ex-wife were both instrumental and monumental in my recovery. I could not have done it without them. It is that simple. After countless relapses, a stint in rehab, more relapses, I just... *stopped*. Even while still living a hop, skip, and a jump from my dealer. It was special. And the more days that went by without using, the stronger I got.

I came to accept my mother's death and learned to process grief as it comes. It has now been almost forty years, so there isn't much grief left lingering. I went through the muck to get here, but I hold onto the lessons for the future because here's the thing about life: *Death is imminent.*

Others have died and people will continue to die. It is the grand prize at the end of the carnival that everyone gets. So as to not fall into old habits, I always keep those lessons close. Always. I have withstood three massive tidal waves and continue to not only swim but move forward. I understand what triggers me and what progresses me. I realize that I simply do not need drugs to enjoy life or to numb anymore. I have come to undoubtedly grasp the fact that, when all is said and done, I am enough. And wouldn't you know it, the very oddest thing happened as soon as I began feeling this way—a beautiful new sun appeared. Gabrielle came into my life.

This is not to say that I don't have nights here and there where I get excited and have one too many cocktails, but it never goes beyond that. And now I have a partner— and, finally, myself—to hold me accountable so I can quickly rectify the situation.

I didn't find Gabrielle because the universe was rewarding my progress with such grace and beauty. No, I believe that I was ready for that type of love because I *finally* began loving myself. I was enough and I felt it. I was no longer masking anything or trying to replace anything. Gabrielle came into my life when I was most in touch with myself—any sooner and I fear it could've been another whirlwind. I was able to create that sun that was so diminished after my mother's death naturally and organically. It all came out of the love I instilled in myself. And it was a beautiful thing.

Friendships

"The language of friendship is not words but meanings."
– Henry David Thoreau

Gabrielle

At the core of every good relationship is one very important thing—friendship. Our lives are shaped by them. We lean on them during our lowest times. It is, for some, the very thing that truly makes life worth living. It's our community, our teachers, our supporters...our friends.

I have now lived thirty-six years, and I have had many different friendships. Some have withstood many years, a few tears, trials, and tribulations, and are still strong and intact. And some came, served their purpose, taught the lessons, and departed from my journey to take another path out of my life. One thing is for certain: The company you keep can shape you into the person you are. *Choose accordingly.*

I want to take you through a few different friendships I've had over my first three and a half decades. There have been so many important ones it was hard deciding which to write about. Some of them I know are reading this book. Some of them might not even know I'm an author or know anything about me anymore. But I truly appreciate each and every one of these friendships and the purpose they've served in my life. None of this is written to hurt feelings, expose anyone, or do anything other than illustrate the lessons I've taken from the people I've called friends. So...here we go.

My earliest friend is someone I no longer speak to anymore. I have nothing bad to say about her. I still think of her. In fact, there have been many times over the years I've missed our friendship, which blossomed in kindergarten and lasted until sophomore year of college.

The day my dad passed away, her mother was one of my mother's first calls. They were there within the hour. I will forever be grateful for that and the love I was shown over many years by her family. We had an endless number of playdates, sleepovers, make-believe games, and vacations, and lots of mischief and fun. She was more than my very best friend, she was my sister.

Violet was the ideal child. She got straight A's, was a star athlete, and never got into any serious trouble. I distinctly remember, when my rebellious phase started and I became far more interested in the boys roaming the halls than any subject being taught in the building, my mother saying during one of our fights, "Why can't you be more like Violet?"

Violet and I rarely fought. In high school, we had different friend circles. She was with the athletes, I was with the cheerleaders and Josh's friends. Still, we never lost touch and continued to maintain our friendship.

Then she started dating *him*.

From my and many other's perspectives, this is where things started to drastically change. Violet had never been into drugs or even alcohol. Once, when we were teens on vacation with my family, Violet and I were hanging out with my college-age cousins and their friends. She texted my mom and ratted on them for drinking. She was what every parent hopes their child will be like in high school.

He was much edgier, not a great student, and he partied. There were nights during the summer after my senior year when I would see her at a party and she was under the influence. Of substances and of *him*.

Then, after Josh and Ryan died in the car accident, I was faced with the loss of another important person in my life. Although Violet and I weren't running in the same circles, and we had grown further apart since she'd entered into this new relationship, it was always unspoken that we were sisters and had each other's backs. So when her mother called me late one night, I answered.

"Gaby," she said as I picked up.

"Hi, is everything okay?"

"I need you to come to the house right now. I don't know what's going on."

I left my condo and drove over to the house I had spent so many nights of my childhood at. Just as I was about to knock, her mom opened the front door.

"Thank you for coming. I...I don't know what's going on."

Violet came barreling past her mom to greet me.

"Gaby! You're here! Where are Josh and Ryan? Are they coming?" she said with a smile on her face like we were heading to Disneyland.

I stared blankly at her for a moment. Then I looked to her mom. She had no words.

"What?" was all that came out.

"Call them and tell them to come over and hang out!" She was completely serious.

"Violet...Josh and Ryan are..." I looked at her mom again, then back to her. "Josh and Ryan are dead."

"Oh, stop it! Call them! Come on, let's go to my room!" She grabbed me by the arm and pulled me inside.

In her room, one of her sisters tried to fill me in on what was going on...which was that no one knew what was going on. It was like something in Violet got unplugged and couldn't be rebooted. And although our friendship would last a few more months, that was really the night I lost my sister.

At first, I tried to understand what was happening. I went over all the time, hung out with her, invited her places...but it just wasn't the same. It got increasingly difficult to hear her talk about my dead boyfriend as if he would be arriving any moment, especially because this was only a few months after the accident. Still, I stayed and tried to find a new way back to our friendship.

Then, one day while I was over at her house, she left for a period of time while I was hanging out with her sister. When she returned and I went to collect my things from her car, my purse was gone. When I asked her if she knew where it was, she smiled and told me that she had gone on a drive and thrown it off a cliff. With my phone, ID, wallet, iPod, and a slew of other things.

Of course, her mom reimbursed me for everything, but it simply became too much for me. When I was with other friends, she would call and text repeatedly. She even showed up at my other friend's house once looking for me when I wasn't there. Her behavior became erratic and scary for me at nineteen years old. So I did what I felt I needed to do to protect myself...I left.

Violet was diagnosed with a mental illness that I will keep private. From what I have heard from her sisters, it's assumed it was triggered by the drugs she had gotten into with *him*. Or maybe it was always there, waiting for her to turn a certain age, I don't know. What I do know is that the support I was trying to give and the friendship I was trying to maintain became toxic for me. It was scary. It was difficult. It was affecting me deeply.

This was the first time I had really been faced with a difficult decision about choosing myself. Most times it's with a relationship gone bad, a shitty family member, or a bad work environment. This was a person I cared for like a sister, truly loved, who now had a mental illness that changed her as a person in so many ways. Every part of me felt guilty and like I needed to stay. It hurt my heart to pull away, but I was nineteen and did not know how to handle what had now become a very toxic and overwhelming situation in my life.

Over a decade later I ran into Violet and her mom at the grocery store. Violet barely spoke, but her mom was very cold to me. After the encounter, I spoke with Violet's sister on social media. What she said to me really shook me to my core.

"In her perspective, you abandoned her daughter the second she got a mental illness."

I felt all of the guilt all over again. And the word abandoned really triggered me. I was also now a new mom and understood the fierce protection a mother has over her child. Knowing that her mother couldn't understand my reasons for pulling away broke my heart a little bit. I sat with this for about a week. I covertly talked about it on my podcast. I lost sleep over it. In the end, I talked about it with my mom, in tears, and what we got to was monumental.

Who am I if people don't accept my authentic self?

It really was the first time I'd had to deal with this notion. Sure, I've gotten hate on social media platforms before from random people behind a keyboard who I'll never see. Sometimes even that has been difficult. But to feel it in a real-life way from someone who was such an integral part of my childhood and young adult life? It forced me to answer the question: Do you stand by your decision?

I do. Is there sadness? Yes. Is there empathy? Beyond measure. But there is also the resounding reminder that her behavior had become unhealthy for me, and I decided to choose myself. It is what I would want my son to do. It is what I would want anyone I care about to do. And I hope it is what Violet's mom would want her to do.

I will always be grateful for the love and memories I shared with Violet's family. They were there for me, just as my family was there for them over the years. I hope Violet knows how often I think about her, send her love, and want nothing but the best for her. And I hope she always and forever chooses her happiness.

My girlfriends from high school stayed through college and are still some of my closest to this day. Sarah—who in the very early days dated Ryan, who was in the car with Josh—has been through the darkest depths with me. I remember after Josh died, my mom and stepdad had to leave town the following weekend. My mom almost canceled, but I assured her it was okay to leave. Sarah promised her she wouldn't leave my side, and she didn't. She slept over, went everywhere with me, and when I mustered up the energy to take a shower, she sat on the bathroom floor and talked to me. She was there through my divorce and to ask me what the hell I was doing breaking up with Tay, and we transitioned into motherhood together.

To sit here and tell you about all the meaningful friendships I have in my life would take more pages than this book has—which is ironic, because my circle is actually quite small. As I've gotten older and busier, and have become a mother, there are fewer people I choose to spend my energy on. Whether it's a friendship that has stood the test of time since first grade (hey, Bordeleau) or the adult friendships that have brought me solace (I'm looking at you, Alex), the ones who still know what is going on in my life when I take a break from social media—I love you.

In 2023 two monumental things happened.

I became a mother.

And I almost lost my best friend.

I've always hated the word best friend. In middle school, it's like, okay, but who is your BEST friend? You can't have more than one. Which is bullshit. You absolutely can. And I do. However, IF you had to rank them on a stupid imaginary scale, my best friend, for all intents and purposes, is "Jess."

Yes, Jess from *Eat, Pray, #FML*.

She was a bridesmaid at my first wedding, she was my first call when I found my ex-husband's affair receipts, she has helped me move houses at least four times, and she did not leave my side when I was going through my divorce. She is selfless, hilarious, loving, and, like me and so many of my long-term friends, has some serious dad trauma that we have bonded over.

Like so many of our stories, mine included, this all started with another *him*. I don't need to go into the details or list the reasons why I did not approve of the relationship—both of them would acknowledge how toxic it was— but it got to a point where I was yet again faced with a now not-so-foreign decision...*to choose myself.*

Jess had developed a problematic relationship with alcohol. Did she drink every day? No. But when she chose to drink, her sadness and unresolved trauma would creep up from the depths she stuffed it down to, and the only thing that could ease that pain...was more. She would drink to excess and then have irrational feelings of hopelessness and wanting to hurt herself. And who would she call when she was standing on the edge, teetering back and forth? Her best friend, obviously. Me.

I want to underline that this was not something that happened every week or even every month. It was random and spread out so that neither of us even recognized the pattern at first. Until 2023, when I was very pregnant, very emotional, and very vulnerable. A fight she and her boyfriend had gotten into was so bad it ended with Jess swimming in an alcohol bottle that became too overwhelming. She ended up in the hospital.

I vividly remember the first conversation we had once she was released. Where I was, how her voice sounded. It started off with pleasantries. How are you, what are you doing, have you seen this bullshit on TikTok? Then I spoke my truth. *I love you, but you can't keep doing this to yourself. You have to be sober. You have to leave him. What can I do to help you?* The conversation ended with us agreeing that she would not call me when she was drunk anymore, and that she would go back to therapy and get her life back together. I think that experience had scared all of us, including her.

They broke up for a little while. Then got back together. And the cycle started all over again. It's so easy to recognize it when you're the observer, but even she was beginning to see it. Jess was on a toxic Ferris wheel of super highs and awful lows. She just didn't know how to get off the ride.

It all came to a head five weeks after my son was born. Tay and I had asked her to be his godmother, and it seemed as if her relationship had found some type of stable ground. We even went to dinner with both of them to really make an effort to pretend I gave a shit about this person my friend had disappeared into. The following evening, they went to a dinner where alcohol was involved, and I received a call the following day. Jess was still drinking. Hysterically sobbing. Not wanting to be here anymore.

I stood in my living room with a five-week-old in my arms. Tay's aunt (a therapist with a specialty in substance abuse, ironically enough) was visiting from out of town. I was fresh off finding out my stepdad had cancer. My husband's back had gone out, leaving him immobile for a week, and it was one of the scariest times I can remember. *And* I was dealing with all the postpartum hormones.

Yet, here I was, on the phone with my best friend, begging her to get in an Uber and leave their apartment before *he* got home. It broke me. The amount that I was trying to emotionally handle added on top of the hormones I was experiencing was too much. I remember I looked at Tay with tears in my eyes and said, "Aren't people supposed to be taking care of *me* right now?"

I knew I had a decision to make. It was either allow this toxic behavior to continue, or to choose myself. I remembered my relationship with Violet. It was difficult. Jess would be ten times more difficult. But you see, now it wasn't just me I was choosing—it was my son.

I told her that if she continued to stay in the relationship that we would have to take some time apart. I think it was jarring for both of us, to be honest. We had never had a fight or disagreement in all our years of friendship. She thought I was saying, *It's me or your relationship, make your choice.* But what I was really saying was, *I will not allow my family to be hurt by this relationship. I choose myself.*

What was so hard was that I knew she was struggling. I had always been her lifeline. Her call. But I have lost too many people I love in this life. For me, stepping back was a shield to protect myself in case I lost her at her own hands because of an inebriated decision. And I will do everything in my power to keep my son from experiencing that type of grief.

It's true that since my divorce I have become more ruthless. I have a hard line, and when you cross it, I'm gone. Forgiveness? Sure. Staying in the situation? No. Part of that I'm sure is to protect myself from the hurt I've experienced in the past...but it's honestly a quality I'm proud of. I am extremely loving, understanding, and supportive—just not at the expense of myself.

After six months of not speaking, except for a few emotional conversations, we had a long talk and set clear boundaries for how we would try and repair our friendship moving forward. It happened slowly, and at one time, I didn't really see how we would ever get back to normal. She missed five precious months of my son's life and that weighed heavily—on both of us.

If my friendships have taught me anything in this life, it is that the ones that are meant to stay will either respect your choice to choose yourself or never make you choose in the first place. Part of me was scared to let Jess read this before publication. The other part of me hoped that it would wake something up inside of her, the strong and amazing human I know is in there, and give her the strength she needed to walk away from the abuse and toxicity.

I sent it to her to read. When I asked her if she had a problem with anything I had written about, her answer surprised me: *Write whatever truth you need to show people they don't deserve the toxicity and abuse so they can get out.*

One week later, she left the relationship.

Jess got back into therapy and moved in with Tay and me for a while. Slowly but surely, we repaired our friendship. She bonded with my son. And after a few months it was as if no damage had been done—or so I thought.

The following year, I invited Jess to join me on one of my FML trips. I have recently been lucky enough to fly to some incredible destinations where I meet a bunch of my readers, bond, travel, and, ultimately, heal, in a way that can only happen when you're finally seen by others who have been through similar things in life.

What I thought would be an incredible experience with my best friend of eighteen years would end up being the very thing that removed her from my life...forever.

From day one, my energy felt like it was being pulled to making sure Jess was happy and okay instead of where it was meant to be—showing up for my readers who were taking time away from their families, spending their money, and looking forward to this experience *with me.*

The cracks were probably barely visible to the girls on that trip...but they were cracking, first at a surface level, and then much deeper. The first happened when we were traveling on a bus from one city to the next. I had been leading a game, keeping everyone entertained and having meaningful conversations, while Jess sat quietly in the front seat, headphones on, in her own world. Yes, the trips are a lot of energy. There are amazing fun times and inevitable heavy conversations—that's why everyone is able to bond and heal the way they do. It's why I love them, and Jess and I had spoken about that element at length.

Finally coming out of her alienated bubble, Jess decided she wanted to DJ. She announced that she wanted everyone to stop and listen to the lyrics of her current favorite song.

I knew the song, and I knew the group of women I was with did not have any business listening to it. It was a ballad about the female vocalist's life basically ending when a man devastated her. It's the type of song you hysterically cry in the mirror to or play as you drown your sorrows with too much wine. Not the vibe for a group of women looking to heal. Not the vibe for this trip.

In hopes of salvaging an awkward situation and relating the weird choice to something relevant, I announced to the girls:

"This is the song Jess thinks should be used for the break-up between Javier and Gabrielle if the book ever becomes a TV series!"

Then, the first deep crack was created...well, rather, *shouted*.

"SHUT UP!" Jess screamed at me.

In front of thirteen women whose lives were affected by my work.

Thirteen of my supporters.

Thirteen of my fans.

I could take pages to further illustrate uncomfortable moments that followed on this trip (that she was a guest on, for free). About her drinking, embarrassing me in front of the women, or being flat out rude to me in private—but instead, I'll take you through the moment when the cracks deepened beyond repair and the whole foundation came crumbling down.

A few days after we returned home, I called her to have a conversation.

"How do you think the trip went?" I asked, trying to broach the discussion with open-ness for an honest talk about what the hell had taken place in Costa Rica. I don't know what answer I thought I'd get—but I can tell you the response I received was the absolute last thing I had prepared myself for.

"I just think the trips are kind of...*unsafe*."

The only response I could manage to get out of my mouth was...

"What?"

"I think it's an unsafe environment. People are coming on these trips and trauma bonding, and there's no professional to then support their mental health."

I could not believe what I was hearing. The entire message of every book I've written, my podcast, my presence on social media, and now, these trips, has always been very clear: *love yourself before anything else, and love yourself enough to heal.* I preach mental health awareness. I've screamed it from the mountain tops. And I'd been on the front lines of *her* mental health journey for over a decade.

The conversation went on for about thirty minutes. I found myself having to explain to my best friend that I've always publicly said I am not a doctor, nor a therapist, and that on the four trips that had taken place, women had had nothing come from it but positive experiences and amazing friendships. I quickly realized it had little to do with the trip itself, and it became very clear that this person had a very different opinion of me than she once did.

"Your love for me is conditional."

When I asked how this could possibly be after the number of times I had stepped up, saved, protected, and been there for her, the response I got illuminated what was really going on.

"You told me if I ever got back with him, I couldn't live with you anymore."

Let me be so clear. Yes, I absolutely said that. That is not conditional love—that is setting a boundary to protect my child, who is now my number one priority. No one comes before him. Not my mother or my husband...not even myself.

"You don't ever make me feel like I can speak up."

This one struck me. I had been deep in postpartum hormones and had been dealing with more on my plate than I ever had before. There had been days when I felt frustrated and emotional—but I never directed it at her.

"That's awful. I never want to make you feel like you can't tell me how you feel. You're my best friend. How have I done that? Can you explain a time when you felt shut down?"

There were no examples.

Still, I apologized if that had been taking place.

After roughly thirty minutes, both of us in tears, apologies on both ends, we said I love you and hung up the phone.

I let a day pass. I reflected on the things she'd said to see if there was anything I needed to take accountability for. But ultimately, there was one thing I just could not get past.

I sent her a text, telling her I was thinking about what she had shared with me, but I could not get past the fact that this person, my best friend, was calling the bonding, healing, magical experience I had worked so hard to create something that it flat out wasn't. I sent her the definition of a trauma bond. *An unhealthy emotional attachment that develops between a victim and their abuser.* This was, unfortunately, what happened with Jess and her boyfriend. This was not, however, what took place on the trip. Bonding with other women over shared past experiences and similar traumas is not trauma bonding. It is finally feeling seen and understood for what you've been through, and that leads to *profound healing.*

We went back and forth on the topic until she told me that I had proved her point brilliantly—she should have just stayed quiet because clearly all I wanted was "yes men" in my corner.

Then she blocked me.

A month later I called her mom to let her know we had a box of things she'd left and to tell her to please bring our house key back when she came to get them. Jess must have unblocked me because I quickly received a message instructing me not to involve her mother "in this" and to leave her things outside. After she came and picked up her things, which we'd left on the porch, she then texted Tay that she had thrown our key out weeks before.

My best friend of eighteen years, the godmother to my son, our family...just...*threw* my house key away? It was clear whatever narrative she now had of me in her head was the one she wanted to continue believing.

Tay and I were now done. We both blocked any communication moving forward.

Remember what she said to me when she had first read this chapter: *Write whatever truth you need to show people they don't deserve the toxicity and abuse so they can get out.*

The truth is, after eighteen years of *willingly* being on the front lines of her mental health journey, this finally opened my eyes. I had been so consumed with trying to get her out of a toxic relationship, I hadn't realized that I was now in one—*with my best friend.*

Suddenly, stories surfaced from my other friends about her rude behavior toward people at my book launch (you know, the book where she is largely written about as my best friend). Repressed and excused memories reemerged of her getting drunk at my celebration dinner and hysterically crying the whole way home, forcing me to take care of her instead of celebrating myself. Boundaries that were continually crossed, like not calling me if she wasn't sober, that I pushed to the side because "it's Jess."

You see, when you're in something so familiar and comfortable, you're not scouring the playing field for red flags—you just expect them to be green like they always have been. I don't know if it was my career, seeing the change in others firsthand on the trip, or my becoming a mother that changed Jess's opinion of me. Or maybe it was easier to discard our friendship, like the key to my home, than accept the thought of never getting back with her ex—because deep down she knew that they could never coexist together.

The day Jess left my life I felt a weight lifted off my shoulders. Part of me feels ruthless for saying that, but it's undeniably true. I am so thankful for the support she showed me in her own way throughout the last eighteen years of our lives. I will remember the laughs and the good memories for what they were. But I cannot deny that the moment I decided to choose me, and ultimately let her go, it felt as if my entire nervous system finally set back into place. I slept better. Huge opportunities presented themselves. It was the familiar feeling of the rose-colored glasses coming off and finally seeing clearly again.

Friendship break-ups can often be more difficult than the end of romantic relationships. No one—no matter how many years they've borne witness to, how many memories of yours they hold, or how painful the goodbye might be—no one can stay at the cost of your peace. *It is simply too expensive.*

The lesson to choose myself has been learned many times. Through friendships, work environments, romantic relationships, and family dynamics. It is a lesson that I brought with me into my relationship with Tay. He knows where my line is, that he can't cross it, and what the consequences are if he does—kids or not. He respects the lessons I've learned, what they've taught me, and the value I now place on my self-worth. So, my friends, I leave you with this: How can you ever be self-*less* if you don't choose your-*self* first?

Taymour

Anyone who has known me for a long time will agree with the following statement: I am the sum of my friendships and relationships. The friendships I have fostered have all gone with me on my journey through self-discovery and will continue by my side through my future. They have quite literally shaped me and saved my life. I lean on them in my darkest times, and I celebrate with them in my grandest times. As I grow older, I realize that our time on this planet is just too damn short, so my motto has become "Enjoy life to its fullest and spend quality time with the ones that you love." Family and friends alike.

I have had the very rare fortune of being with a group of friends for close to forty-five years. It has become so uncommon in today's society that it's hard for people to even believe. They are the kinds of friendship stories you see in the movies that for many people don't feel attainable in actual life. The connection I have to these seven friends is truly that of a storybook. Hence, their story, in this book.

It was 1980, in a suburb just north of San Francisco, and I was gearing up for my first day of kindergarten. Little did I know that, on that day, I would start relationships that would last my lifetime. The group started out that day with six and grew by two in the subsequent years. We are eight strong and every one of us still alive...which is also somewhat rare. Many have tried to join our beloved circle throughout the years, but no one lasts, and as we get older, our clasped hands tighten to create an even more impenetrable circle and bond.

When I say friendship, I really mean brotherhood. We have been through thick and thin. Our experiences could fill entire books, so it's hard to summarize in just one chapter the significance a group of guys can have on you. Zack, Carl, Tony, Jamie, Ben, Joe, and Matt—each one has created their own sound in my symphony of life. And we continue to make musical memories as each day goes by.

In high school, we dubbed ourselves "The Posse," and we hung out every weekend. We all ventured into different friend circles throughout the years, but we always ended up back at our roots, together. Today, the majority of our communication is on a blistering text thread called *The Boards*. But when the stars align, we all still get together, and those times are filled with constant laughter and fond reminiscing.

Rather than picking some of the epic stories revolving around these fellas—such as getting lost in the woods on mushrooms or barely escaping wild boars or saving our dogs from wolves while camping—I think it best to pick two of the monumental moments in *my* life and focus on my friends' impact on me during them.

The passing of my mother was significant for a multitude of reasons. Especially *when* it happened—a time when I was most vulnerable and raw. The first year of my teens brought with it death and sadness. Thirteen was too young to bear such a tragedy but old enough to feel it through and through. It gave new meaning to the slogan *thirteen going on thirty,* and I probably wouldn't have made it through without my core group of friends. They were all there for me at any given moment, but there was one friend that emerged out of the group and stood by my side during my roughest period and is still standing there today.

Zack was arguably the anchor of the whole group, for we always found ourselves at his house to swim, and it was Zack who I had the most sleepovers with. My mother used to call him her second son, before my brother came along. Zack was always there. He came to all of my family functions and on all of my family trips. Everyone in our group called each other best friends, but Zack and I were inseparable from the very beginning.

I remember it so clearly, even though it was thirty-seven years ago. My goodness, trauma sure has a wicked way of imprinting on our memories, as if somehow burning itself into our very DNA. My mom went down on a Sunday afternoon. By Monday afternoon, the whole town knew about it.

That first night was a nightmare. The hours of waiting at the hospital while they ran tests felt like an eternity. My young mind couldn't comprehend what was happening, let alone process the possibility of not having a mother. I was lost. Once we learned that it was a severe brain aneurysm and there was zero chance of recovery, the focus shifted to misery and saying goodbye. My world had turned upside down in the blink of an eye and the only place I could think to look was to my friends. That first night, all I could muster was a phone call to Zack, informing him of what had happened. I remember that phone call vividly. I cried openly, and so did he. That's the thing about Zack. He is so open that his compassion for others makes him vulnerable, and it's beautiful. He really makes you feel like you're not alone.

He immediately felt what I was feeling. It is also not lost on me that he was losing part of his childhood as well. My mother doted on him just as much as she doted on me. She loved him tremendously, and I know Zack felt that love and subsequently the absence of that love when she left us. To this day, it was one of the more pivotal phone calls I have ever had in my life.

The next day, the plan was to go back to the hospital to see if there was any progress. I remember that morning being very bleak, and why would it be anything but? We did not get the news we wanted to hear at the hospital. We then headed to San Francisco International Airport to pick up my beloved Aunt Elaine, my mother's sister, my *Mama Goose*. My grandfather Harold was also there. He was the quintessential grandfather, whom we lovingly called Pop-Pop. He wielded a tobacco pipe wherever he went and wouldn't be caught dead in public if he wasn't wearing something tweed. I loved him very much and as much as it was a comfort to see both of them, we were all aware of the circumstances we were navigating. They were preparing to say goodbye to a sister and a daughter painfully too soon. This shit sucked for everyone involved and there was no faking it. There were very few moments during this seventy-two-hour period where I was even able to take a breath without a tear threatening to fall. It was as if I was in some sort of tailspin that I couldn't get out of. I tried to think of something else, anything else. I thought of what my friends at school were doing. Were they just going about their day normally? Did they know what had happened? Had Zack told our group? Unbeknownst to me, every teacher at school had made an announcement informing everyone of what had transpired.

It was about 11 a.m. by the time we returned from the airport. We had been crying the whole drive back, and I had finally fallen asleep in Mama Goose's lap as my dad tried to explain what the neurologists had told us the night prior. It was maybe the first time I had slept in twenty-four hours. As we pulled into Marin General Hospital, I realized that the last time I was at the hospital was three and a half years prior for the birth of my brother. Oh, how cyclical life can be. This day wasn't filled with tears of joy and welcoming new life. This day was quite the opposite.

I vividly remember the sun shining down through the entrance as I walked through the glass doors. There were a lot of people moving about. It is almost coming back to me like a dream sequence as I write. As my eyes looked past all the people moving in front of me, I managed to make out a still pair of sneakers, the only ones not moving or shuffling about. I smiled because as soon as I saw the sneakers, I knew who they belonged to. Zack. I gasped and screeched out, "ZACK!" and we ran into each other's arms.

We were thirteen-year-old boys running at each other and hugging like Sylvester Stallone and Carl Weathers in Rocky III. But that was the thing. It was pure, unabashed love. True friendship. We both started crying pretty heavily, and from that moment on, we were attached at the hip. I don't think either one of our young souls was ready to handle something like this, and we instinctively leaned on each other for support and guidance. I said I am the sum of my friendships, and this is the perfect example of that.

Zack saved my life in a way. He was there for me. In the blink of an eye, my mother's warm sunshine vanished and I was left in the cold, dark, and scary void for the first time. The second I saw Zack that morning at the hospital, I felt the sun shine on me in a different way. He assured me that I wasn't going to be alone and that friends could and would make it all better. He taught me at such an early age what a friend is, how to be one, and the value and saving grace they can bring to your life. Yes, Zack is the anchor of our group...and it's because of moments like this.

Each one of my friends from *The Boards* was there for me in one way or another when my mom passed away. And as we grow older and lose more loved ones, I am and will continue to be there for all of them. But it isn't only in death that friends make their most important statements. Sometimes, they come to you when you are at your most vulnerable. Your most scared. Your most sick.

As you read in the addiction chapter, I spent a good portion of time lost and wandering around the bottom of a barrel. I was an addict and that's all there was to it. But through all three waves, there was one constant friend that either shared in my misery with me or became a beacon for me to clean my act up.

His name was Tony, and he was one of the founding members of "The Posse." He was also the one I spent the most time with during my twenties to forties. He was an actor and a force to be reckoned with when it came to performance, and he took it very seriously. I have him to thank for ushering me into my own passion for the craft. Tony moved to New York soon after college and was on his way. I looked up to him not only for his talent but his ambition. He was a highly motivated young man, and it was infectious. You really should've seen him on stage. You couldn't take your eyes off him, and I had the utmost pleasure of producing and starring in a play opposite him, which was a dream come true. To this day, I look back on that production of *American Buffalo* as one of the proudest moments of my career, even though it came so early on.

I will say this right here and now—I owe a good portion of my life to Tony, and not for the reasons you may think.

Yes, he introduced me to acting, and for that, I am eternally grateful. He showed me something that created a fire inside of me that has lasted my lifetime. I have channeled all of that creativity into every art medium possible, from painting to music to acting to directing. I owe all of my creativity to Tony for igniting the spark that first created it, that internal big bang. But that's only half of the reason why I owe him my life.

When I was at my lowest point in life, Tony was there the whole time helping me through. Drug addiction can take down the best of them, let me tell you. I've seen the strongest of them all be wiped off the planet from drug addiction. In fact, Tony, had he not straightened up when he did, would've been another statistic. He had a terrible addiction as well but fought his way through it and out the other side. He was a few years ahead of me in recovery, so when I was in the thick of it, he was clean and sober. Reminiscent of when Zack stood by my side after my mom passed away, Tony stood by my side, held my hand, accompanied me to meetings, and did whatever he could to help guide my way through it. He showed me mercy and gave me hope when I was dry of it all. He stuck by me even when others had one foot out the door. His resilience and his patience impacted me so strongly that I was able to make that change once and for all. And so I was taught the lessons of loyalty, resilience, patience, and, above all, what it truly means to put in the work with someone. I have brought all of those lessons into my relationship, and I accredit my successful marriage to them. I am so grateful for that. Most importantly, I was taught a lesson that would help soothe the ever-present wound of abandonment that had been left on me years before—sometimes, people don't leave. Sometimes, people stay.

Like Zack and Tony, all of my close friends have been there for me in one way or another. And vice versa. These relationships make this life a better place and create a loving space inside my heart to accept what life brings, good or bad. If I wasn't the sum of my relationships, I don't believe I would be as good of a partner as I am, or as good of a father. These friendships taught me patience, kindness, and respect, the same ingredients that I bring to my relationship with Gabs and my relationship with my children.

It is safe to say relationships and friendships alike are put in your life for a reason. Some to mirror you, some to challenge you, others to teach you, comfort you, love you, and some to break you. And on very rare instances, a person enters your life and encompasses every single reason known to man. There is one person in my life that fits that bill—my brother Tavahn, the most magical idiot savant there ever was. In fact, we have dubbed him the Idiot Tavahn-t. He is one of those real pain-in-your-ass types that you can't help but love immensely. The type of person that can severely trigger you in one breath and make you want to start a business with him the next. There is no person on earth that has experienced more of life by my side than he has. Yes, Gabs and my children get more of me now, but my kid brother and I have been palling around for forty years.

It is pretty impossible to sum up a relationship with a sibling in a few paragraphs, so suffice to say we have lived quite a life together. I could tell you of our heated arguments or periods of time when we didn't speak. Or I could bore you with stories of brotherly bonding over a joint and a bottle of Jameson. We aren't special, we are just two brothers doing our best to survive in a world that is filled with carnivals and fun houses.

Tavahn is brilliant in most things he does and, now that my beloved Uncle Rock is no longer with us, he would hands down be one of my lifelines on *Who Wants To Be A Millionaire*. He never graduated high school yet managed to get accepted into a reputable music school in Los Angeles by sending in a demo tape of his band—on which he played every single instrument. To me he is a virtuoso, although he would deny and deflect it all, saying that I only feel that way because I love him so dearly. I have looked up to my younger brother for years, and I am definitely not ashamed to admit it. He has a natural talent in whatever he puts his mind to, and it is infectious. I don't always subscribe to his way of thinking, and we have had our fair share of missteps in our relationship, but he is my brother and I will always *love* him...even if we don't *like* each other sometimes.

One thing that will always remain is his soft chewy center. He's very compassionate and loving and generous, just as my father and I are. He also has the same fire and passion that we have. The apple definitely didn't fall far from the tree and probably hit my apple on the ground upon falling. We are all cut from the same cloth, and I would like to think that I had at least a little part in instilling those ideals and morals in him at a young age. When we were suddenly dealt with the loss of our mother, Tavahn was only four years old and unaware of the world and all its blunders. I took it upon myself to love him and cherish the ground he walked on so that he would feel the same love I felt from our mom. That devastatingly sad time in our lives became a time of purpose for me. It became a time for me to raise this young man the very best I knew how. At least for the next four years until I was off to college. I didn't put my high school experience on hold, but I did put my brother first in a lot of situations. I felt bad for him, even though he was most likely too young to realize the severity of life at the time. I looked to him for laughter and warmth, and in each other we found our future.

Tavahn will always be someone I can undoubtedly rely on to make decisions for the good of both of us. He has become a pillar of mine, like Mama Goose and my mother-in-law, Dee, have, and I find solace in the fact that together we will rule our little world with smiles and laughter. That little shit loves to laugh.

I would be remiss if I didn't include my relationship and friendship with Gabrielle, my North Star, my beacon. She and I have developed a relationship that is the strongest bond I have ever had with anyone. It isn't all the big things that make us special in my eyes. It isn't the careers, the marriage, or even the parenting. It isn't the sex, or the attraction, or even the goals we have. No, it isn't the big things that shift your life within relationships. In fact, it's quite the opposite. It's the little things. It's the light and the fun. It's the laughter and the joking. It's the unspoken stuff like quietly holding space for the other when they are down. Making yourself available to their triggers and trauma brains. Pulling your weight without saying that you're pulling your weight. And mark my words here and now, those are the things that will be responsible for our longevity. It is these elements of our relationship that our children will relish and pass along to their young. This life, this world, is far too short to be worried about the big things. Let's sit in a field of little things that make our world go round. That is where we will find our biggest solace and our greatest love. There is a quote from Rumi that states "Out beyond the ideas of wrongdoing and rightdoing, there is a field. I'll meet you there." Well, *this* is the field I'm talking about. A green meadow-like field without a preconceived notion of right or wrong. Just us, laughing and joking and living and loving. When I'm with Gabs, I'm in that field—and it is where I want to stay.

Living in a field like that, in a relationship like I am in, has transformed me into the exact person I saw myself growing into. I always saw a future for myself, I just didn't know how I was going to get there. It wasn't until I met Gabs that a passion was stoked inside of me. I wanted to live happily with someone while mutually holding respect for one another. She made me want to grow up and grow up I did. I've strived to get rid of some of the petty arguing tactics I held in my previous marriage. I still work on respecting her boundaries around alcohol and my behavior surrounding it. On the rare occasion we do fight, we go to counseling. When we don't see eye to eye, we compromise at every turn, and we are always leading with love. Remember what I started with—I am the sum of *all* of my relationships—and there is no other relationship more intrinsically intertwined with my own spirit than Gabrielle's.

As I grow older, I find myself reflecting on my friendships quite often. The impact they have had on me at every turn shaped the person I have become and, moreover, the person I am shaping my children to be. I value those friendships greatly as I know they don't come but a few times in this short life. The older I get, the more value they hold. It comes back to one of my core beliefs—this life is but a blip on the radar, so spend it with the ones you love. I find comfort and solace in the thought of sitting in that green field with my family and my group of friends, just laughing and enjoying each other's company. Not sure what you call that. Some might call it a dreamland. Others might call it the other side. I call it heaven.

Divorce

"Maybe part of finding what you wanted was recognizing what you didn't want."
– Claire Cook

Gabrielle

Tay and I were both absolutely *dreading* writing this chapter. While it is such an obvious life-changing time in each of our journeys, it is not always fun to dive deep into the pool of what didn't work. However, we were both dreading it for very different reasons. Tay is currently in the other room finding out what I know all too well—how uncomfortable it can be to write your truth about something that others might not agree with. I did this in both my books, with people who I didn't need to keep any type of a relationship with, much less a healthy one. To write your truth about your divorce when you need and want to keep a healthy friendship with your co-parent? I do not wish that on anyone—and good luck to my husband on his half of this chapter.

Since I chose the name Daniel for my ex-husband in my first two books, it seems only fitting we stick with that name. After all, that is what I call him to this day when talking to my friends and family. It is the name he booked all of his affair hotel stays under. The name his second phone was registered to. It is also, come to find out, what his nineteen-year-old girlfriend knew him as for the first six months of their relationship. Until one night on vacation with her family, he passed out drunk and she found his license in his wallet—with a name that was very much *not* Daniel.

I want to be extremely clear about this: After packing my things and leaving the house I shared with him, I very quickly became detached from that relationship. Quite frankly, those five years of my life with him feel as if they never happened. I went on to discover in *Eat, Pray, #FML* that I was never really *in love* with Daniel. I married him because he was (ready for the irony?) *safe*. When I tell you he has become just a character in my story, I mean that wholeheartedly. I would gladly sit down over a cup of coffee (preferably with my podcast mics present) and discuss his perspective on how he became a seemingly different human overnight. If you're reading this, Daniel, my number is still the same—let me know if you want to come on the show.

Indeed, this chapter has proven to be the most difficult to write. Not because I'm scorned and angry at him. In fact, I continuously count my blessings that the marriage ended before it wasted any more years of my life. It's difficult because I am so incredibly exhausted of talking about this human. Could I have written an entire book on the ins and outs of his criminal activity once my first book blew up? Yes. And a Lifetime movie. But I have no interest in continuing to write about someone who is so far removed from my life. So when I knew we were going to do a chapter on divorce, I sighed, rolled my eyes, and thought...what do I *actually* want to say about it?

I'm often asked by people if there were any red flags. Any signs. *Did you have any idea who he really was? Did you see it coming at all?* At the time, and even for a while after, I would have said no. I was totally blindsided, as was everyone around me. Now, after a Europe trip, a broken heart (to his dismay, *not* by him), and a shit ton of healing, I can see there were most definitely some grenades and red flags flying in my face that I chose to ignore. So, for this chapter on divorce, I'd like to take you back to the beginning, in hopes someone reading this can get out before it's too late. And to let others in on a little secret that society doesn't want you to know...*you should be proud of your divorce.*

I suppose the first red flag I ignored was the fact that Daniel was incredibly uncomfortable with my career. Yes, it is a normal human emotion to not be totally fine with the fact that your significant other is going to be making out with someone in a movie, and I completely understand that. But it was so much deeper. I will never forget being on the set of a film where I was seen as "one of the names" for the first time. I was making more money than I had before in my career. It was the best and worst experience all wrapped into one week of shooting. I had a scene where I had to kiss the lead actor (who I'm still friends with, love dearly, and who is wildly happy...*with his boyfriend*), and my first night on location, we had a welcome dinner. I got a call from Daniel, and I remember the panic setting in as I rushed away from the group I was having dinner with to answer. After a few minutes of pleasantries from my then fiancé, the conversation took the turn it always inevitably did, starting with seemingly innocent questions.

"Who are you having dinner with?"

"Cool, who are you sitting with?"

"Has anyone hit on you?"

"When do you have to shoot *that* scene?"

This was the same exhausting conversation we had already had fifty times. I remember just trying to appease him and keep him calm, anxiety filling my insides while I tried to smile and look happy so none of my castmates knew what a mess I was currently floundering in. Then I offered the piece of information that I *thought* would rectify the situation—or at least calm my future husband down.

"Daniel, he is the nicest guy, and this is his first movie. And he's very much *not* into women."

Why am I telling you all this? Because the next thing that came out of Daniel's mouth was so incredibly absurd it should have knocked the engagement ring right off my finger. It will also hopefully illustrate a very prominent flag that is the color known as fucking *red*. I apologize for the graphic profanity in advance—his words, not mine.

"Cool, and how do you think that makes me feel knowing he sucks dick and is kissing *MY* future wife? So when you come home and kiss me, it's like having a bunch of dicks in my mouth."

...

Did you just let out a laugh at how ridiculous that is? Good. Let's continue.

"Well, Daniel, I too have sucked some dicks in the past. So I guess that's what a toothbrush is for."

While this is all hilarious and insane to reflect on, there is a point to me reliving this very embarrassing conversation. Insecurity is a normal human emotion. We've all experienced. As is jealously. It's something we as humans are faced with and need to recognize and learn how to deal with. *This* was a different level of insecurity. Jealousy. Obsession. *This* was a huge red flag flying in my face. *This* was a very good example of someone being *SO* focused on something, *SO* triggered by something that it highlights something within *them*. Daniel was hyper-focused on the fear of me cheating on him while I was away on set. Even if I didn't have a make-out scene with someone batting for the other team. If I had *any* male castmates that became friends, in his mind I was *for sure* hopping into bed with them the first chance I had. *That*, my friends, was shining a light onto a part hidden within *him*. Because he knew, deep down, he would be hopping into bed with a variety of women the first chance *he* had.

One time in therapy our therapist straight out asked him the question: Why don't you support Gabrielle's career? His response was simple and succinct, and I have never and will never forget it: *Why should I? It's not like she's ever going to make it.*

There I was, sitting in a therapy office that we were paying a lot of money to be in, fighting for...*what?* For my significant other, who had met me when I was an aspiring actress, to just simply...*believe in me?*

Alas, my abandonment wounds were too deep. I hadn't yet gone on my life-changing healing journey and recognized the fearful scars I had been carrying with me since I was a little girl. So, of course, I was going to cover my eyes, pretend the flags were a romantic shade of passionate pink, and do everything I could to make sure this relationship was *the one*. Yes, Gabrielle was the fiery, strong, twenty-seven-year-old who everyone saw on the outside. But little six-year-old Gaby who lost her daddy was really the one running the show. So... be with the person who would continuously say he was sorry, shower me with gifts, and promise me he would change? Or be by *myself*? At the time, the latter was more terrifying than who my ex would eventually become.

Looking back on this now it is so clear—this was me abandoning *myself*. Allowing someone to treat me this way, manipulating my own brain into thinking it was acceptable and fixable, and simply *not* choosing myself. At that time in my life, there was nothing more terrifying than being abandoned. The thought of it immediately put me into fight-or-flight mode. Luckily, my divorce was the catalyst for me ultimately starting to heal my abandonment wounds.

When I returned home from Europe, with a still-fragile heart and many memories, the biggest lesson I had learned was very clear: *I'm never truly abandoned because I will never abandon myself.* It wasn't until I saw how fully capable I was on my own, and really, how much I loved being on my own, that I was able to decrease the fear of abandonment. When you don't have the fear of the big scary monster in the closet, you can simply walk past it and out the door. I had learned the lesson of choosing myself in my friendships. It was now time to learn it in the romance department. I knew I would never again compromise my own happiness just to be safe in a shitty relationship.

My career was simply one example of the cracks that existed long before Daniel and I walked down the aisle. Once his affair started (unbeknownst to me), suddenly other cracks that I had never noticed began to appear.

"You should dye your hair blonder," he said to me one day. "Like the Barbie blonde you used to do in high school. It's so hot."

"I won't work with my hair like that." I laughed. "I audition for the girl next door, the tough chick, the girl from the wrong side of the tracks. Not the hot chick."

Then came the random suggestions of how good I would look if I got my boobs done. Let me be SO very clear—even now, breastfeeding my baby, I cannot WAIT to get back to having little boobies. I am a loud and proud president of the itty-bitty-titty committee. So, luckily, these suggestions were always met with a laugh.

Or the ever-fun conversation about money that eventually turned into flat-out manipulation. If you're reading this and you think being an actress in Los Angeles means you're rolling in the dough, let me burst that bubble for you. You're stoked if you're making $125 a day on an indie film. Sometimes you book jobs, sometimes you don't work for months. It's a super-fun career for a type A with anxiety.

"Look. I know you've been stressed about money lately, babe," he said to me one afternoon in the kitchen. "If you ever decide you want to be a stay-at-home wife and just, you know, lunch with the girls and work out...I'll take care of everything."

I looked at him, waiting for the catch.

"But if you want to continue working and acting, then I think it's only fair you take care of your half of things."

Ah. There it was.

What seems like a careless douchebag comment on the surface was actually so much deeper—and so much darker red than the other flags. This was the first attempt to control me financially. This is why so many (mostly) women cannot get out of toxic marriages even when they decide they want to. Because if I didn't have money or a support system, how could I have ever chosen to leave when I discovered the cheating? I continued to pay my half of things until the day I left the home we rented.

Years later, I would hear from his girlfriend's friends that she was desperate to (please understand these are *not* my words I'm about to quote...) *"escape him."* He was her manager. He controlled her social media accounts. Her money. Her life. There was, quite literally, no way out. This was after the Barbie blonde hair and boob job.

I remember after countless sessions, fights, tears, make-ups, and false promises, I was *still* fighting for the relationship to work. I was still looking for the final push to leave. After all, I had just had a fairy-tale wedding that my mom had worked her ass off to give me, had made a commitment to this man, and had said till death do us part. And so this brings me to a very important point I want to make in this chapter on divorce—*you do not need a reason to leave.*

For whatever reason, society has made us feel that we need to have some big valid list of motives to end a marriage. Why? If you are in a long-term relationship that you are no longer happy in, it is perfectly acceptable to decide you want to leave. Sometimes even applauded. If you're not fulfilled at your job or not making enough money and your passion lies elsewhere, no one shames you for making a switch. So why, just because we got all dressed up, said some fancy words, and made it all legal, should we be shamed into staying in something that has become unhealthy, toxic, or just unhappy? I am in no way saying that marriage should not be taken seriously—it absolutely should be entered into with pure intentions of committing to that person. I am simply saying you should never stay in anything, no matter what it is, that makes you dim your light in this world. You should never sacrifice your happiness—life is too long and too short all at the same time.

The freedom I felt after watching divorce papers be handed to my ex-husband and the physical weight I felt lift off my shoulders when I drove away from our home for the last time is a memory I hold close to my heart—because it is a moment I didn't listen to the judgment, the shame, the told-you-so bullshit of society. It was simply the first time in a relationship that I had chosen me—*and you never need a fucking reason to do that.*

That one small moment led to a whole lot of healing. It led to me having the courage to take my *Eat, Pray, #FML* trip, which completely changed my life. It was the start of me healing my abandonment fears. It was the first massive chip knocked off the giant iceberg of trauma and the beginning of the lessons I was about to learn. Finally, after sinking to the bottom of the deepest part of the ocean, I came up for air. Turns out, my divorce was exactly what I needed to begin the journey back to myself...and now it sure feels good to be floating happily on the sunny surface.

I am more grateful for my first marriage than most probably know. Was my wedding a massive waste of money? Yes. But I will say, I produced the *shit* out of that event. And even still, I look back on it fondly—because all my girlfriends, my family (some who are no longer here), and so many genuine people really showed up for me that day—*we just cast the male lead entirely wrong.*

Even though those five years of my life truly feel like some weird fever dream, the lessons I took forward from the relationship, the marriage, and the divorce have guided me to the healthy and secure marriage I am proudly in now.

How would I so clearly know what I *do not* want if I hadn't made those mistakes? I've experienced someone who did not support me, wanted to change and control me, and ultimately made me completely dim my light. Having that experience and feeling that low let me know that I will never allow myself to be in any type of relationship—romantic or other—that makes me feel that way again.

They say you need to experience the lows to appreciate the highs. This is a prime example of that. The support and safety Tay makes me feel in our relationship is so deeply appreciated because I have experienced the polar opposite.

How else would I have learned what to *never* accept? And in turn, know how to accept a healthy love that would never abandon me—because I finally knew I was the one person I needed all along. My divorce taught me how to undoubtedly and fiercely choose *myself.*

Can you grow and heal in a relationship? 100%. There are times I can feel Tay and me growing and healing both together and as individuals. For me, it wasn't until I chose myself and walked away from my toxic marriage that I truly started to heal and grow into the person I wanted to become—and so much of that needed to be done alone. After healing those parts of myself, I was able to attract a person who mirrored me—safe, healthy, and ready. So for those of you reading this who have not yet found your person, let me ask you this: *How can someone else undoubtedly choose you if you haven't wholeheartedly chosen yourself?*

Nothing I am writing about now happened instantly. There was a period of time I felt embarrassed. I felt like a failure. I felt the shame our culture intends for you to feel. And I want you, if you're going through this now or will be in the future, to know: *Those feelings are completely normal.* Allow yourself to feel it—to grieve it—to sit in it as long as you might need to. And then after the wine and ice cream, and maybe a trip to a foreign country and a drunken mistake or two, remember the words written here.

You do not need a reason to leave.
You are simply choosing you.
You are a badass.
Be proud of your divorce.

Taymour

Have you ever seen *Pee-wee's Big Adventure*? Right. Of course you have. But if there is anyone reading this book who has not seen this timeless classic, put the damn book down and get some fucking culture in you. Okay, sorry. But really, it's a must. There is a scene in the movie where a pet shop is on fire. Pee-wee, played by the incomparable enigma that was Paul Reubens, keeps running into the burning building to save "all the animals," but every time he passes the snakes, he can't do it. He's too afraid. And I can relate—I fucking *hate* snakes. I will protect my wife and kids from anything, but if there is a goddamn snake on the ground, they better run faster than me. Kidding, but I really do hate the little serpent bastards.

Pee-wee passes the snake aquarium numerous times, side-eyeing the snakes with other animals in his hands as he scurries from the fiery blaze. The last shot is of him running out with two handfuls of snakes and then passing out from fear. Ha, a brilliant moment in movie history if you ask me, but I digress. Pee-wee knew that eventually he would have to get to the snakes, even if it meant he had to do something uncomfortable. The point of the story is that this chapter is the snake aquarium for me. It is, in fact, the last chapter I am writing and the one I least wanted to write. It goes back to that responsibility in even writing this book. This isn't just self-journaling over here. People are going to read this. Important people. And feelings are at stake. So I want to take accountability. I want to be honest. And I want to hold space in my heart for the feelings of those close to the story.

Let's quickly dive a little deeper into the relationship I was modeled growing up. As wonderful as my family life was, there is a flip side to every coin. And my family was no exception. My mom was a Scorpio, my dad was a Scorpio, and I am a Gemini. If you're not into astrology, then let me just say, the fact that we didn't burn the house down is a fucking miracle. There was some serious passion and fire. My parents were wild, and that is putting it lightly. I was a witness to it every single day, as was my brother once he arrived. They were wild in love and wild in anger. My mom and my dad would fight like there was no tomorrow. I guess a better analogy would be they would fight like their kids weren't watching. Oh, but I *was* watching. I have the therapy bills to prove it. Look, I can't sugarcoat it. It was intense, but it was a different kind of intense. It was passion. It was love. I'm not saying it was healthy or non-toxic. Especially for me, a young boy in my adolescence, just trying to figure it out. But there was something about it, something other-worldly, something scary, and I couldn't take my eyes off it.

One of the more extreme occurrences that I remember happened around the dinner table. The two of them got going and it escalated to the point of them chasing each other around the table, yelling and screaming. One second, my mom was chasing my dad and the other second it was the other way around. Just like a freaking cartoon. But unlike the cartoons, they wanted to literally kill each other. Just then, my mom grabbed a fork and continued the chase, only now a weapon was involved. I was eleven.

My mom finally made it around the table, and just when I thought she was going to kill him with the fork, they fell to the floor and began kissing. I was crying uncontrollably so they brought me down to their level and we all just lay there for a while. This was normal in my household. This was my definition of love.

Divorce fucking sucks. Let's start there. No matter what the circumstances may be. At one time in your life, you loved that other person with absolutely everything you had. So whatever the reason that brought you to this decision, the underlying feeling we are left with is *this fucking sucks*.

I met Katy in my early twenties at one of her music shows in a bar in San Francisco called Hotel Utah. She was a friend of one of my childhood best friends, and I fell in love with her the very second I heard her sing. The way she commanded the guitar, her voice, and the audience was astonishing. I, too, was exploring my creativity in the arts but she had it down. Her confidence while performing was just crazy. My creative outlet was acting, but performance is performance, and she was something else. After her show, we immediately hit it off and didn't leave each other's side for three straight weeks. I could feel the potential for something amazing. Potential being the operative word. I was not ready for something serious, so I slowed it down and decided we should just be friends. In fact, we stayed very close friends and were still somewhat inseparable. Fast-forward to her doing the music for a film and getting me my first acting job in Los Angeles. We had both moved down here as friends, at one point even living together but never taking it further. It was the easiest relationship I had ever had with a woman up to that point. We had a lot of energy those days. We were creative together and we were fun. We eventually moved to different houses but remained fairly close. We each had our respective relationships, but we were always there for each other.

Then one terribly fateful day, I received a phone call that practically stopped time. It was Katy, and I hung on every word as she told me with waning strength that she had been in an ATV accident and had broken her back. My heart dropped. After the shock subsided, she explained that she could still walk but there would be significant rehab. So, of course, I was going to step in and take care of her as much as possible. It was regular doctor visits with dinners and a movie to follow. It was easy and enjoyable, and I felt so sorry for the position she was in. What I was not expecting in the least bit was to fall in love with her while she was laid up in a massive back brace for months. Nor was she, but fall we did. And as our love grew, her back began to heal and we started living a normal life together.

While the majority of our early time together was fun and carefree, there were definite red flags that neither of us were accepting. Things would pop up and we would move past it. There were just some fundamental differences in our personalities. We did things at different speeds. What she thought was romantic, I though was somewhat annoying, and vice versa. These are things that sincerely don't bother you at the beginning but slowly eat away at your soul as time moves on. Under the rug we swept those red flags and in two years we were getting married, not realizing there were a bunch of crusty red things piled up underneath the surface.

When I got down on one knee in Yosemite, she hesitantly accepted, then spent a few hours questioning whether or not that was the right choice. I'd always had an issue with her struggle to commit to a decision, and this was certainly a massive example of that. An extremely hurtful one, I might add. If that's not a red flag, I don't know what is. The following morning, we headed back toward Los Angeles in a huge argument. We came to the juncture where if we went right, we would go to Paso Robles to save our relationship. If we went left, we would go back to Los Angeles and break up. We went right. Romantic? Maybe. Toxic? Hell yes.

Here's the thing that I now so clearly realize. That chaotic type of love reminded me of the crazy, unhinged, and often unhealthy highs and lows that I witnessed with my parents. During that time in my life, I hadn't yet uncovered that belief, so I simply convinced myself that it was all part of the romance I was so desperately seeking. Let me let you all in on a little secret that has changed my life and well-being: *Love doesn't have to be chaotic to be passionate.* Love can be exciting and thrilling without the toxicity I was finding in so many of my relationships.

My lessons hadn't been learned as of yet, and there I was, marrying my best friend. Behind the unnoticed occasional toxicity, life was somewhat magical. We lived in Hollywood, in a wacky loft that was a dream space for two creative types. I was auditioning and bartending regularly, while she was playing music in and around town. We were mid-thirties artists trying to make it. We were financially struggling every step of the way, but we made it fun. We traveled around California as much as possible and really enjoyed spending time together. We were happy and in love. Other than adding the occasional red flag to our growing pile, everything seemed to be going in the right direction, so we both decided that it was the perfect time to have a baby.

Ten months later, she was giving birth to our daughter, Juniper. It's clear this little soul was supposed to make her entrance, and she did so right before the foundation of our relationship began to crack. Juni was perfect in every way. But even her perfectness could not stop the divide that was growing between her parents. After Juni was born, Katy and I began shifting our focus away from each other. Our bickering and disagreeing turned into fighting, and we were finding it difficult to see eye to eye on most things. It really was a collapse on all fronts.

There wasn't any one thing that ended our relationship. There was no cheating, or violence, or stealing, or even lying. As meaningless as it sounds, the straw that broke the camel's back, in my eyes, was her not being able to decide which color we were going to paint our walls. Four different color swatches lay on that wall for what felt like an eternity. (In reality, it was probably three months.) The fear of commitment that initially hurt my heart after proposing had come back full circle to end what we had been building, in the form of fucking paint. By then, we were not happy and it was beginning to show in front of Juni. I definitely take a lot of responsibility for that, but we were both guilty of it and neither one of us kept our side of the street completely clean.

We had gotten into a pretty bad fight on the way home from our Christmas holiday in the Bay Area. We had left early so I could get back in time to start working at this hot spot in Los Angeles for New Year's Eve. This fight was different than the others. I couldn't tell you what it was about, but I could tell that both of us were done, as could she.

The plan was for her to move out for a while to see if that helped in any way. You know, get a little separation happening so we weren't right on top of each other. We began seeing a couple's therapist, but nothing seemed to work. I remember saying to myself that if we were going to divorce, then we should do it soon, rather than waiting until Juni was old enough to really understand it and be affected by it. So it was me that went ahead with keeping the trial separation going and moving toward divorce.

Here is where I must be clear in telling you that I always wanted marriage to be forever. I honestly saw Katy and I growing old together. I would've never married her if I hadn't. But that clear image began to fade, and there wasn't anything I could do about it. There were never other women, and I had not started using again. I was falling out of love, and it was a weird, hurtful, feeling. Because know this—I still loved her very much, but it was the same kind of love I felt for her the whole twenty years prior to us getting married, in the friendship we probably should have just stayed in. Thank God we didn't, because look at what a beautiful little soul we created...and I wouldn't have it any other way.

Much of the story you've heard up until this point is kind of cookie cutter, no? Leave it to me to add in the heavy drama. What slowly started on that fateful New Year's Eve bartending gig with a few bumps here and there to ring in the New Year manifested into another major drug wave. And as you read in the addiction chapter, this was the one that almost took me out. Shortly after we separated, I began using regularly. I would use on the nights I was working, because I would work until 5 a.m. and then not use when I had my daughter. Terrible, but it was my only job at the time, and I now had to cover the other half of the rent since Katy had moved out. I'm not saying I couldn't have done it without drugs but, as we all learn in addiction therapy, we find reasons to use. I didn't possess the strength or the know-how to get myself out of it at the early stage. Katy eventually caught on and what started as concern for me, her daughter's father, turned into fear for her daughter and rage against me. All warranted reactions to what I was going through and subsequently putting her through. And, as much as I hate to even write the words, what I was *putting my daughter through*. She was so innocent, and I kept all of it from her, but there is no way she didn't catch on to my shift in spirit, no matter how good of an actor I think I am. And for that, I am eternally sad. I have made up for it in my own ways, but I think that until she is of the age when I can speak to her about it all in honesty, it will forever just linger there for me.

I'm not going to lie, the divorce started to get ugly. Our separation and eventual divorce lasted for about three years. There were attorneys involved but thankfully there was no court. Gabrielle often jokes and gently reminds me how patient and lenient Katy was during this whole time—and that if it were her, she would have left, with my kid, without looking back. And I am grateful to Katy for that grace. There were some random drug tests, which occasionally set us back due to my relapses, but once I was committed to my sobriety, we started to work toward a healthy and peaceful coexistence.

I was finally committed to my health, my daughter, and my life. I was finally back on track. It should be noted here that, coincidence or not, it was at this point when Gabrielle was reintroduced in my life, and we began our journey.

Although Katy and I were in fact separated when my madness sprang up again, it still doesn't take away the pain I put her through during this time. It is one of my big regrets in life. I don't regret much, but the way I handled my health, her feelings, and my daughter's parenting when she was between the ages of two and four is a huge one. I am constantly working on forgiving myself for that—and writing this chapter is another step in doing so. Regret and forgiveness are funny in that you can't forgive yourself if you don't fully understand the regret. But to understand the regret, you must first comprehend why you did whatever it was that you regret. It's a process that takes a clear mind, time, therapy and...more time. Processing it all leaves you with a clearer path to your own happiness. So process it all I did, and my life began to shift ever so slightly—to my relationship with Gabrielle. I would've never been able to withstand a relationship with Gabrielle had I not done the work to forgive myself and live without regret. It would've been much the same as all my prior relationships. I was truly and absolutely discovering myself for the first time in my life, and it was a beautiful thing.

During Covid, Katy and Juni embarked on a three-year move to the Hawaiian Islands. Some major finessing and understanding took place during that period of time, on both our parts. Katy and I have begun to navigate our way back to being cordial co-parents and are doing our best to be friends. We now reside in the same town and share love and responsibility for Juniper. We have come a long way and we have many years between us, but there is the one common denominator that will always connect us—our commitment to our daughter.

Together we stand, trying to make her life as grand as possible, and for that I am grateful. It's not to say that we don't still have our differences, which at times turn into bigger things. But as time goes on, I can safely say that Katy has defined her space in my heart and spirit, and it is there to stay. I can also safely say that, if I have a heart attack, it probably stemmed from that same space. Jokes aside, and Gabrielle and I relish in this often, we couldn't have a better human to be co-parenting with, and Juni is all the better for it.

So, yeah, divorce sucks. For everyone involved. No matter what. But it is what we do with it thereafter that counts. There can be green pastures in the future, it just takes a lot of work to get there. Once the pain subsides and the drama dies down, we should be asking ourselves:

How can it teach us to be better people?

How can it teach us to love differently?

How can it teach us to look deeper within ourselves to make a difference?

If we can come out of all of it with a better understanding of our own inner workings and of the human experience...then divorce served its purpose.

Birth of a Child

*"Sometimes the smallest things take up
the most room in your heart."*
– Winnie the Pooh

Gabrielle

It is hard to put into words all of the things a child brings into your life. There are the obvious ones—less sleep, more responsibility, and a large dent in your savings account. Then there are the things that make it all worthwhile. The newborn snuggles that feel like you're still one entity. The little sounds they make when they're dreaming. Seeing something that is a perfect combination of you and the person you love looking up at you. It's true what they say: Having a child is like watching your heart walk around outside of your body. It's beautiful. Magical. Frightening. All-encompassing. And boy, has this tiny human already taught me some massive freaking lessons.

As I sat in the waiting room of my OB's office with Tay, really swollen, incredibly uncomfortable, and definitely over being pregnant, I wished she would hurry, the fuck, up. Was she actually late? Who knows. It very well could have just been the fact that it had been many months since I had made eye contact with my vagina, and I was currently in third trimester hell. It's a special type of torture, being nine months pregnant in the dead of a Los Angeles summer, a torture I wouldn't wish upon anyone. Well...maybe my ex-husband.

She eventually graced us with her tiny frame and New York flair, complete with some expensive designer shoes that she deserved a medal for committing to for an office day.

"Your blood pressure is a little wonky today, how are you feeling?" she asked, looking over my chart.

"Fine. I mean miserable, but fine," I answered.

She plopped some clear goo on my very large belly, and we saw our little alien appear in black and white on the monitor beside us.

"Looking good in there! Although he is sunny-side up. He still has time to move."

"What's sunny-side up mean?" Tay asked.

"He's in the right position, head down, he's just looking up toward the sky," she explained. "Have you had any headaches?"

"Yes, actually. A few over the last two weeks."

Her face changed. "Hm."

"What?" Tay asked nervously.

"I'm sure it's nothing, but I'm going to send you across the street to get some tests. If anything comes back, we may induce you today, but most likely I'll see you next week."

We headed across the street, not thinking too much of it, assuming we would be on our way home soon and still able to make our dinner plans with friends at Olive Garden. Hey, you know, pregnancy cravings.

That is not what happened.

After a bubbly young nurse took my blood pressure in triage a few times, she looked quizzically at the machine in front of her. A few minutes later, my OB appeared.

"What are you doing here?" I immediately realized what this all meant.

"Just checking on everything." She calmly clicked around on the computer screen next to me. "Your blood pressure is all over the place. So, we're gonna take him out tonight," she said casually as if my unborn child was a pre-made pizza.

"WHAT?" Tay said, shocked.

"Yeah. Everything's fine, he's just making you sick in there. And he's fully cooked so let's take him out! After I get back from the Taylor Swift concert."

Long pause.

My OB was a *die-hard* Swifty, and it was the final night of her huge tour. When we first met with my doctor, she had told us that by the time my due date rolled around she would 100% be in town because, by then, her kids were back in school, and she wasn't going anywhere. The ONLY day she said she would not be available was in fact that very day—which at the time wasn't a concern, considering I wasn't due for another week and a half.

She clicked some buttons, signed a form the nurse was holding, smiled at Tay and I, and said, "See you tomorrow morning!" She floated out of the room to join TSwift for a night of friendship bracelets and eras.

I glanced over at my somewhat-pale husband, who looked like he'd just been told the 49ers were no longer a football team.

He raced out of the room to get all the essentials needed for the next few days. They started me on a magnesium drip for my blood pressure, and I made a few phone calls to important people to let them know what was going on.

This was the first lesson my son so graciously decided to teach me: *You have zero control.* I have always been a bit of a control freak. For the nine months during my pregnancy, my mother would laugh and say, "If kids will teach you anything it is that you really have no control. They run the show." Well, please take your seats because my son decided the show was about to begin...ten days early.

"Side effects of this can be headache, nausea, and feeling very flushed or dizzy, so let me know how you're feeling," the nurse said to me. I was sure I'd be fine. I never really have side effects. I felt fine. Everything was going to be totally fine.

A few hours later I found myself in our private room, puking into a little hospital barf bag, peeing myself in the bed because I had zero pelvic floor strength, and fighting the worst fucking migraine I had ever had. It was, in fact, not fine.

I looked at Tay around 3 a.m., weak and exhausted from the endless cycle of icing my head, puking and peeing, and dragging my new appendage, the IV, to the bathroom and back.

That night (and the entire three days in the hospital, really) gave me an entirely new respect for nurses. I mean, I've always respected them, but now I think they are God's gift on earth. Jocelyn, who was our first night nurse during my very glamorous *fluids from every end* party, was like a literal angel taking care of me.

After I finally fell asleep for a few hours, I was on the other side of the side-effects hell train. They started me on the medication to begin the induction (since Miss Swift had taken her final bow and my OB had given the green light) and things began to progress. A few hours later, I felt a gush between my legs and thought, *Oh shit, am I just uncontrollably peeing right now?* My water had broken. It was go time.

Around four centimeters, my fabulous-as-ever OB entered the room to give us a detailed play-by-play of the concert to make sure we knew that Taylor Swift was like the Beatles in the sense that *We're all just lucky and blessed to be in her presence, you know?* Awesome, Doc. *Shake it off* and all but can you get this fucking baby out of me, please?

As she was giving us the lowdown on her favorite part of the concert, I had a contraction. I started to breathe deeply and turned on my side to hold onto the rail of the janky-ass hospital bed.

"If you're in that much pain already, you can get the epidural whenever you want."

"I want," I replied. I was perfectly capable of breathing through the uncomfortable stabbing pains as they came and went, but I was *not* interested in finding out how much more intense they were going to get.

When Jesus arrived (and by Jesus I mean the epidural man, who looked freakishly like Ryan Reynolds), they sat me up and got me prepped to stick the giant needle of *I don't want to fucking feel anymore, thank you* into my back.

As Deadpool numbed me, I looked at Faith, the nurse who had taken over early that morning, and took a deep breath.

"So, I think I'm gonna pass out," I said casually.

"Oh. Okay," she said, grabbing both my arms to steady me.

Faith and the Green Lantern laid me down on my side. Luckily, he had gotten the epidural where it needed to be before I decided to check into dreamland. A few minutes later, I was a very happy pregnant woman who could no longer feel anything from the waist down.

Let me tell you about drugs. Wow. I thought an epidural was meant to help ease the pain and make everything more tolerable—no. When I tell you that for the rest of this labor and delivery journey I felt zero pain, I mean I literally felt nothing. The contractions just...stopped. For those women who choose to bravely embark on this journey of creating new life and opt to not have this magical little drug—I salute you. I think you're fucking crazy, but I salute you.

About two hours, a few cups of Jell-O, and a matcha latte later, Tay and I were laughing, listening to some calming music, and still contemplating what the hell we were going to name this human that was about to enter the world. Then, it was time.

I started pushing. About halfway through, my OB informed me that he wasn't coming out without a little more room.

"Do you want me to snip you or let you tear?" she asked.

"I DON'T KNOW JUST DO WHAT YOU HAVE TO DO TO SAVE MY VAGINA" was my response. She snipped. And no, I didn't feel that either.

Tay held my head. We'd had many discussions of where he would be standing during delivery. Most of them went like this:

"You cannot cross the threshold. Most women poop on the table. You can't be down there."

"But I caught my daughter when she came out!" he'd protest.

"Yes. And you guys are now divorced."

He'd concede.

Happy to report he abided by the set agreement, and we are still married.

After thirty-six minutes of pushing and my face feeling like it was going to spontaneously combust, we welcomed our son into the world.

Now before I talk about this next part, let me be clear: My OB had no idea what line of work I was in nor did she know anything about my books or my and Tay's journey. For those of you who haven't read *The Ridiculous Misadventures of a Single Girl*, Tay and I call each other unicorns. Cheesy? Maybe. But, you know, love and happily-ever-after shit.

Out comes a seven-pound baby with a MASSIVE gelatin-like bump on his forehead. It literally looked like his brain was misplaced on the outside, and if our doctor hadn't been so chill about it all, we might have panicked a bit. Instead, she smiled, held him up like a little naked trophy, and said:

"You have a unicorn baby!"

Both our mouths dropped open. Of all things she could have said, the fact that it was *that* sentence let me know what a powerful little being had just entered the world. *Buckle up, Mom and Dad. I have arrived.*

Buckle up, indeed. There is nothing that can truly prepare you for having a child. I had every hot ticket item from my registry purchased and set up in the nursery. I didn't know how the hell to use most of it, but it was all there ready and waiting. We had taken a few classes. I had watched too many TikTok videos. *Nothing* will prepare you for when you put them in their car seat to leave the hospital, and the nursing staff just waves and says, "You own a human now, good luck!"

I recently read that if you have a daughter, you're meant to heal generational trauma in your life. If you have a son, you're meant to heal trauma men have inflicted on you in *this* life. I have no idea if there's any truth to this, but WOOF does that track for me. And let me tell you, I thought I was all happy and healed in life and my relationship with Tay when I decided to get pregnant, and my son promptly said, *HA. That's funny, Mom. Let me show you what's up.*

My son has been a constant reminder to stay on top of my thoughts. Every trigger and wound that I have healed— abandonment, heartbreak, fear of death—were all now suddenly thrown back in my face. What if someone abandons *him*? What if some bitch breaks his fragile little heart? What if Tay dies and I repeat the same cycle my mom did, and my son is left without a father, and I just have to...figure it out?

What if another man I love...dies.

What a horrific intrusive thought, am I right? Welcome to a trauma brain, where you play out in-depth scenarios of potential ways this could happen to the tiny little human you would throw yourself in front of a moving bus for. I've had to *constantly* stay on top of my thoughts to redirect them to create what I want, and not allow past wounds and fears to dictate my (or his) future.

I've experienced what it's like to take on the fears of your parents. Witnessing my mother go through things in my childhood that I now realize I need to work through as an adult. That is something I'm sure is inevitable in some capacity, but I don't want to create that for my son. *He* shouldn't grow up with a fear of the people he loves dying. *He* shouldn't be afraid of being abandoned. Yet, how am I to teach him the opposite if I can't fully know that myself? The answer, I'm afraid, won't magically appear. It brought me back to the same fear I had before deciding to date Tay— *but what if he dies? What if something bad happens?* I'm proud to say, I walked through those fears, and thank goodness I did. That is the only reason I was able to recognize my intrusive thoughts around my son and redirect them. I truly feel that he is here to reprogram that trauma for me— to show me a different outcome, where everything is okay.

With some healing came a whole new set of unfamiliar fears. Ones that are beautiful and terrifying all at the same time. As I sat in the rocking chair with his three-week-old self on my chest, he slept peacefully, occasionally stirring to lift his head, stretch, and collapse back down. It's exhausting being a baby, after all. I suddenly realized I needed to start memorizing every single thing about him. His features, his little movements, what his face did when he startled in his sleep...because it finally hit me...what they always say. The daunting realization that he will never be this little, ever again. And with that, my heart filled up and broke all at the same time. Welcome to motherhood.

A few days later, I was pushing him in his stroller on one of our nightly walks. I had my Trevor Hall playlist on shuffle, as I usually do, and the song "You Can't Rush Your Healing" came on. Just a few years earlier, I was walking the streets of Pai, Thailand, lost, listening to these lyrics penetrate my soul while I was trying to heal myself. Now, I was walking the streets of my neighborhood, pushing my son in his stroller, just him and me, hearing these lyrics in a completely new way for the very first time.

The journey never really stops. You're never magically "fully healed." There are always new challenges, with more work to be done, and new lessons to learn. But it is important to take the moments like that—where it is so clearly full circle—to acknowledge that you have shed a past self and stepped into a new one. To recognize that you have grown into someone new, who can hear things that once broke you and realize they now empower you.

Now, in the early wild stages of toddlerhood, a new set of lessons have arrived. On one hand, I feel as if so many of my experiences prepared me for parenthood. On the other hand, some days I stop and think: *Seriously, they just **let** people be parents?*

Navigating the ups and downs of the postpartum period is not for the weak. I think sometimes we forget that we ourselves are just little girls all grown up. Little girls existing in this life, simply trying to figure it all out, for the very first time. Looking back at some of what I now recognize as postpartum depression, I wish I would have reminded myself of this. I wish I would have hugged the little girl inside of me the way I hugged my son—because she was healing, learning, and growing right along with him.

Having Tay witness and support me through some very deep spirals caused by hormones has only strengthened our bond. Partly because he bore witness to me overcoming everything that motherhood physically and mentally throws at you like a dodgeball to the freaking face. And partly because in the moments I felt lost, misunderstood, and terrified of the darkness I found myself in, my husband's hand still appeared before me—to reach down into the depths, hold my hand, and help pull me back to the surface. There is healing in finally knowing someone fully has you. There is healing in finally surrendering to someone. And what a journey of healing I've had in this life that has prepared me to not only do that but to wholeheartedly value and appreciate it.

I feel sometimes that life has hardened me. Unintentionally, every abandonment, divorce, heartbreak, and letdown has left a scar that has hardened my once-delicate heart. My son broke all of those impenetrable pieces off the moment he was put in my arms. I had always searched for a man to fill the void my father's death had left in my heart. While some came close, it inevitably was my job to fill it myself—and I did. However, I was always acutely aware that a tiny little patch remained over that spot I had worked so hard to heal. It's true, a man would one day fill that void my father's death left. It just wasn't any boyfriend, fiancé, or even husband. It was you, Stone Christopher Ghazi. You were the missing piece. Not you being born, but the lessons you've already begun to teach me. The softness you've brought back into my life. The beautiful vulnerability I feel when I hold you in my arms. The empathy I now feel for all men, who were once this little and fragile, who maybe didn't have a mother like me that so desperately vowed to protect their heart, teach them compassion and kindness, and show them the way.

That empathy made it so much easier to forgive those who had hardened me—because I knew their little boy inside simply wasn't healed. At the end of the day, having my son was the final piece of the puzzle. To forgive the men who had wronged me, to have compassion for those who hurt my heart, and to know that it was all so incredibly worth it.

With that forgiveness came space. I have more space in my heart now—for my husband, my mother, my child, and most importantly, myself. It allowed me to forgive myself for my own mistakes and missteps along the way because, when he was born, I was reintroduced to the little girl who has now become his mother—and that little girl still has some things to heal. Every single thing you've read in the pages of these chapters was preparing me for this next phase in life, and yet, sometimes, I feel less prepared than I ever have before. Motherhood is the most terrifying and exhilarating freefall I have ever experienced. Sometimes it feels like I can't catch my breath...and other times I think my heart might actually explode from the love I feel looking at his smiling face. When I look back at the timeline of my life thus far, all I can do is be thankful. Because every one of those life lessons, healing journeys, and winding paths...led me to him.

And I would walk it a million more times to find my way to you, my son.

Taymour

There is something so surreal about looking into the eyes of your children. You have the privilege of being able to look into their eyes more than any other human being on the planet does. Your connection with them is irrefutable, and it starts at minute one and lasts a lifetime. It is a connection bonded in genetics and upbringing. A connection that will leave the utmost impact on you if you choose to relish in it—and I do.

I do understand that parenthood is not for everyone, and I certainly respect that. I have many friends who have decided to proceed on their journey without children, and I get it. While parenthood enhances your life in a million ways, one thing it does for damn sure is strip you clean of any freedom you've ever had. Plain and fucking simple. I also firmly understand that parenthood sometimes isn't in the cards for biological reasons, even if desired, and I virtually hug and hold space for you if that is your experience.

For me, being a father was always in the stars—it was part of my destiny. I have felt the need to be a dad for as long as I can remember, even at a young age. Most of that stems from my early years of watching my dad and mom raise me. Maybe it was seeing how my amazing father navigated life after loss, all the while holding space for his children, with the utmost love. He was always my guiding light, my beacon. And the way my parents looked at me and loved me was really like a drug, one that I yearned for and still do. It's crazy how instrumental the first few years of one's life are. I don't think you realize it until you have a child of your own. You see how they look at you and need you, and you return it. It's just pure, unabashed love happening right in front of your eyes, every second of every day, and it's beautiful.

It is also somewhat cyclical in that, as we raise our own children, we are spiritually brought back to our own childhood. I can remember cuddling with my mom or dad and have vivid memories of watching my mom sew while I clung to my blankie. Those memories are from when I was less than three years old, and I started to remember them when my firstborn was between the ages of one and three. Now, again, with my second child, I am vividly remembering things I had otherwise forgotten. Not only are my children keeping me young by bringing out the child in me, but they also allow me to reminisce about the child I was. And viscerally remembering my mother's love for me has certainly helped in healing the loss of her. I also think the realization that I am one of my children's beacons, along with their respective mothers, encouraged feelings of *being enough* rather than triggering my fears of leaving them behind. Although those fears still peek around the corner from time to time.

Looking back, I might not have been absolutely ready for parenthood, especially the first time around. I took a major role in raising my brother when my mom died, so

I had the nurturing and caring parts down pat. Now it was about being ready to pass along my ideas, values, and morals. To instill in my children that we lead with love, but we stand strong in our beliefs. That when we fall, we pop back up and try again. That the wheel of life always spins, so hold on. To respect the life you have been given because it is delicate. To respect death because it is inevitable. But most of all, I try to teach them to be easy and gentle on themselves. Enough hardship will eventually make its way to all of us, so I want to teach them to try to spend that precious time as happy as possible. There is so much in this world and in this life to be happy about...go find it. And finally, as if I could write it in the stars, I want them to know: YOU ARE ENOUGH.

It is certainly not lost on me that I just recently learned most, if not all, of these lessons myself and am still learning as I go. Parenthood is weird that way. I am not perfect, as I have delicately laid out in this book. I am still learning, and I am still reminding myself of these very lessons. Teaching them one at a time as they come, I find reinforcement of my own beliefs, which only strengthens me more, and, in turn, forces me to reckon with what is important to me.

I have had the lifelong pleasure of helping create two wonderful children, my daughter, Juniper, and my son, Stone. It is everything I imagined as a kid and so much more.

Juni, as we lovingly call her, is a firecracker and a fairy all in one. I was there when she was born, and she came out ready to rock the world. Though it was twelve years ago at the time of writing this, wonderful memories of her birth still exist in me. She was born in the very room Brad Pitt and Angelina Jolie's baby Shiloh was born. And get this, it was overlooking the Hollywood sign. Not gonna lie, being an actor and having my firstborn delivered in a room looking directly at the iconic sign was bucket-list shit. Katy, my wife at the time, was almost two weeks overdue. As cool and collected as everything seemed to be, there was some urgency. Katy narrowly escaped a C-section, and thirty-five hours later, Juni was on her way. The nurse asked me if I wanted to actually do the delivering, and I, of course, jumped at the chance and scrubbed up.

Juni was born perfectly healthy in my arms, and Katy and I couldn't have been happier. Like all women, Katy was a powerhouse for nine months and was able to deliver our daughter with few complications. I was so proud of her. As soon as Juni showed her face, I recognized her striking Ghazi eyebrow. It was exactly like mine, and it was the very first connection of so many. It's a magical time but also scary. You are just left with this human being that is completely relying on you to figure everything out, and there is a whole helluva lot to figure out. From the car seat to the swaddling. From the burping to the diaper changes. There is a massive learning curve, but when you love someone as much as I loved Juni, every second of it is worth it. Anytime they make eye contact with you, all of the work and tiredness goes away, and you're left relishing in the fact that THIS is forever.

As happy as we were, the reality of it all set in pretty quick when we walked through the door back home. After we settled in, we had about three weeks until Katy had to go back to teaching, so I was about to be a stay-at-home dad. Don't get me wrong, I was pumped. What eager first-time dad wouldn't want to take on the daunting task of going at it solo? But I didn't know the deep dark depths of humanity I was about to enter. I wasn't warned, and it was something else...something fierce.

I led with love the whole way. On the one hand, you're looking at this cute little being you had a part in creating, but on the other hand, you really just want to take a sip of your coffee, take a shit, or just, you know, breathe. I mean, it's all-encompassing in those first six months, and when you are alone for a large portion of each day, you lose your mind a little. It not only showed me how much I valued my freedom, but also that I needed to mourn the loss of it.

With the loss of freedom came the one thing that is completely undeniable: the true bond you make with your child during that time. They are just helpless little nuggets that need every ounce of your attention to survive, and that is scary for someone who absolutely loved his freedom and way of life. In those early stages, that was a big lesson for me. To be able to just succumb to the love, care, and attention, and push away any feelings of regret about losing the other part of you. As much as I wanted to be a father, I still had career aspirations and goals to fulfill—now I was just gonna have to do it with my daughter by my side. I decided to look at it as a motivator rather than a hindrance. It was time to show her how to enjoy life to the fullest. And in her first twelve years of life, we have developed an extraordinary bond that has never swayed. Not even when I decided to get married and have another baby. In those first two years of Juni's life, I learned the true depth of my love and that I was willing to sacrifice parts of my life I didn't want to sacrifice. I learned a great deal about how visceral the human experience of parenting is and how patience and consistency are key ingredients. Neither of those things made up my stew prior—and both I now know are key ingredients to a healthy relationship. I also learned many great lessons about communicating with your partner. Katy and I did well at the beginning, but patience and consistency were nowhere to be found, so the communication began to wane. Lesson by lesson, I created a path to a better understanding of myself, parenting, partnership, and love...all lessons I remind myself of daily.

Now it was time to bring a little boy into the picture. I was ready and excited. I knew there were going to be some similarities in children, in parenting, and in how I processed it all, but I was also aware that there would be huge differences. Not only in the parenting of a boy rather than a girl, but in my own age and the difference between parenting in your late thirties and forties as opposed to being in your fifties. I did have some anxiety going in, to be honest. I want to be lively and vibrant with my kids...and I'm not getting any younger. Plain and simple.

That anxiety was overwhelmingly drowned out by my love for Gabrielle and my desire to have a family with her, regardless of age and time. No, I didn't want anxiety to be an ingredient in my experience, but it kept creeping up. That is, until about two hours before she went into active labor.

I walked to Starbucks to get her a matcha latte. That walk was one of the most peaceful walks I have ever taken. Something washed over me. I was settled with everything and ready for all of it. I was excited and ready to be a father to a little boy, a feeling I accredit to Juni, to be honest. I was brought right back to that first six months with her and bonding the way we did, and I just began to feel warm. I began seeing the world just a little differently—a little less dramatic and with a purple hue. I had no time to think of age or longevity. All I could think of was warmth and love. The anxiety left me all at once, and I just knew everything was going to be fine. Within two hours, Gabs was pushing. The pushing didn't stop for some thirty-six...*minutes*. It was completely out of this world. She pushed so hard the blood vessels in her face began to pop. Again, I saw the raw and unwavering POWER that women possess. Gabrielle was like a fucking gladiator in there, and it brought me to tears. I well up just thinking about it. Her OB calls her a beast to this day and uses her as an example to her other patients. Low and behold, Baby Stone joined us a few minutes later and all was right in the world. Everyone was happy and healthy, and I was through the roof with excitement.

The connection and love I felt for Stone when he joined us was exactly how I had felt with Juni...immediate and intense. I never wanted to stop looking at him. He was so pure and helpless, and each day my love for him simply bursts. My children being here puts into perspective what is important and what is not. I am balanced when I look into my children's eyes. I am full when they are with me. And along with Gabrielle, my North Star, they help shine my way. Together we live, hand in hand.

Stone's first year of life was a wild ride. Going in, we had been told that parenting boys was totally different than parenting girls. Girls are more likely to be calm and cozy, until they hit the teen years and become angsty and hormonal. Boys are supposed to be hyper and crazy until they hit the teen years, and then they tend to calm down. At least, that is the consensus. Juni, as much of a tomboy as she has always been, was in fact very cuddly and cozy until about...right now. Though still somewhat cuddly, she is twelve and about to hit that teen-year hormonal shift, which is already throwing her emotions in every direction but straight. Stone? Not so chill is this one. The dude is trying to do backflips off the kitchen table when he is not devouring everything in sight. He is constantly trying to mix it up, always causing a ruckus. To quote the amazing John Goodman in the movie *Raising Arizona*: "This one's an outlaw, I can see it in his eyes."

There have been so many significant changes in me in the twelve years between my children, it's hard to tell if the experiences feel different because of the individual child or because of the growth and changes in myself. It seems like a lifetime ago that Juni was born. My outlook has grown more positive, and I am altogether healthier this time around. This isn't just a *me* thing, but as we get older, we become wiser to our own issues and become better at addressing them.

As you will read in my chapter on triggers, I am still discovering, addressing, assessing, and fixing them, but there is something about your children being around you that makes that process move along more quickly. You find solace in their eyes and freedom in your life when they look at you. The perfect example of this is my mornings with Stone. That should be the title of a children's book, and the escapades we share during those mornings seem to come from a storybook.

I get up about thirty minutes prior to him waking, get his morning bottle prepped, and make my quad-shot almond milk latte, cause I don't fuck around. Once I hear him stirring, like clockwork at 7 a.m., I go in ever so quietly, and the second we make eye contact it's giggles, roughhousing, and morning snuggles. Stone and I spend a good thirty minutes just enjoying our time together. I'm now in the process of potty training him in this morning window, which, as tedious and crazy as it sounds, can actually be a real bonding exercise between you and your child. I have made it fun for him, and now I think he looks forward to it.

Leave it to a one-year-old to keep you on your mental toes. I am constantly working to be a better version of myself for Stone and Juni alike. To not fall back on old habits or old personality traits. Someone who accepts his age and let's go of the fear of leaving everyone behind. Someone who stands atop the mountain and claims *I am enough*. Your children, if nothing else, hold you accountable to the issues you are trying to improve in yourself, even if they are none the wiser for it. My perception of them makes me want to be the best, and for that I am eternally grateful to them. It ignited when Juni was born and is now reignited with Stone. The way he looks at me, the way he laughs at me, the way he relies on me is the fuel I need to push through anything. In all of his glorious innocence, he has taught me the most important lesson of all: what my love place is. This is the place we manifest from, create from, and want to spend as much time in as possible. He has single-handedly reminded me of what pure love looks and feels like, all with his silly little laugh. What a gift to be given to spend mornings in a place like that.

The birth of my son was not only life-changing for Gabs and me, but also for his sister. She was so excited to finally have a sibling and so happy it was a baby brother. No one would have faulted her for being jealous or having difficult emotions about such a life-altering change. But Juni couldn't have been more thrilled to have a little sibling. I can confidently and happily say that she is just as in love with him as we are. She has lovingly accepted the role of doting big sister and is extraordinary with him. She actually reminds me of myself with her those first few months. Just in awe and completely in love.

Throughout the pregnancy, Juni was always so helpful and cognizant of Gabrielle's needs and comforts. In hindsight, I think it was her way of getting ready to be a big sister. Her excitement was palpable in the months leading up to the birth. And the moment Gabrielle first placed him into Juni's arms at the hospital? Safe to say THAT particular moment on THAT particular day is in the top three moments of the fifty years I have been alive. To have my daughter and son and wife all hugging soon after his birth was magical. Within ten seconds flat, we were all crying, and everyone was happy.

The birth of your children is monumental. It changes you in ways that you cannot describe until you experience it. The deep connection I feel to both my children is unmatched, but along with that connection comes a deep sense of responsibility. Not only a responsibility to show *them* the right way, but also for me. It brought a severe sense of responsibility to just—*stay alive*. After the birth of Juni, I was overtaken by a crushing wave of addiction that almost took her away from me. It left me helpless, but it led me to a love for my children I never knew I was capable of. I made the adjustments I needed to make. I am so thankful that I can sit here and write my experience, because, for a terrifying moment, it seemed I wasn't going to see the light of another day.

Since those days have become pages of the past, my world has become my children's world, and I live every day to stay here and harness them in that world. But shoot, no one ever told me that with that responsibility comes a million and one intrusive thoughts. You know, the shit that pops into your head when you're trying to go to sleep, like you not being able to get your children out of a fire. What the fuck, brain? Or you and your wife getting into a nasty car crash and leaving them alone in this world. Or planes—yeah, don't even get me started on planes. Coming from a traumatic past, it takes work to keep those at bay. To consider and be considerate of my thoughts more diligently. When they creep in, uninvited, to remember Stone's goofy little smile and return to my love place—my knowing.

One thing I have learned in my fifty years is that life is always too short. Whether a sudden death takes you out early in life or you live until you're ninety, it's still not long enough. That is never more real than when you have children. You begin counting down instead of counting up. Time seems to go a lot freaking faster when you pass forty. All you're left to do is enjoy it—but even that takes work.

Like all my other pitfalls, I had to work to find the root. This incessant feeling of not having enough time directly came back to my relationship with death. It's been tumultuous at times and has left some tremendous scars, but I always come out of the grief knowing that death is a part of life. Again, it's the grand prize every single one of us get at the end of the carnival. And therein lies the lesson—to enjoy the time I'm here instead of fretting about how little or long that time is. Put aside the intrusive thoughts and leave behind the bad choices. Enjoy life to the fullest. *Let your children see you enjoy it.* They will hopefully be infected by it and continue living with all of that enjoyment shining on inside of them, long after we say our goodbye. Juni, my Buggy. Stone, my Chickey Monkey. Shine on, you crazy diamonds. Shine on.

Triggers

"Be grateful for your triggers.
They point to where you are not free."
– Unknown

Gabrielle

Triggers. They can be such a bitch when you don't understand them. So many of us walk around unaware of what triggers us, where it stems from, and we are unable to recognize triggers when they rear their ugly freaking heads. Often, we stumble our way through fights with significant others or struggles with our family members thinking, *That's just life.* Or, *Why did I react like that?* Sometimes it's *They must have some serious issues.* What we haven't been paying attention to, or maybe have just been unaware of (until now), are *triggers.* Buckle up...because they absolutely suck.

First, let's start with what they are. At their core, triggers are unhealed wounds inside of you that are begging to be dealt with. Think of them like a little ninja inside your spirit—and when something familiar feels dangerous to you, your little ninja jumps to attention and starts doing an unnecessary amount of karate kicks and chops, making your heart race and blood boil to protect you while you go into full-on flight-or-fight mode. So fun, right?

While they definitely don't feel comfortable when they're happening, I assure you, triggers can be incredibly valuable. When you're conscious of them and recognize them, you have a direct map to what inside you needs to be worked on. Remember the game Operation? The little man where you had to pick out bone pieces with a tweezer and if you touched the side it made some god-awful noise? Triggers are like that. Hear the awful noise, find the pain point, and be directed to exactly what you need to fix. It's that easy.

Except it's not easy—because this all happens when you're in the heat of the moment. Your brain starts wigging out to try and protect you, and you end up in either a huge fight or a pile of tears.

I'd like to take you through some examples of times I've experienced triggers—some monumental and others barely big enough to notice—in hopes of showing you how they can lead you to pain points within yourself that are simply crying out to be loved and healed. So...here we go.

Let's start with the examples that are very easy to illustrate. The night Josh died in the car accident, the last text I received from him was: *I'm leaving now, I'll text you when I get home.* He never did. To this day, if someone tells me they're going to call or text me at a certain time and they don't—whether it's Tay, a friend, my mother—I automatically assume they're dead. Dramatic? Maybe. Trauma brain trigger? 100%. It's crazy what the brain will come up with when you allow it to run wild once triggered. Instead of the logical assumptions that they fell asleep, don't have service, or are busy doing a million other things, they are *obviously* lying in a ditch somewhere, never to be heard from again, and I should probably start planning my life around how I will move on from such a tragic and traumatic event.

If you haven't ever been through a trauma that has caused intrusive thoughts, you probably think I'm a crazy person. If you have, which I bet is the greater majority of you, you're probably laughing out loud while reading this because it's so fucking relatable—and I'm sorry for that.

More recently I experienced an all-too-familiar trigger in a wildly new way. Tay and I had begun sleep training Stone. (Please, save your opinions and just focus on the story—each family should do what is best for them.) Any mother will tell you how absolutely horrible it is to hear your baby cry—and Stone was not really a big crier. In fact, unless there was something majorly wrong, he didn't cry much at all for the first few months of his precious little life, and when he did, he was soothed very quickly. The sleep training method we used (and were coached through because I was quite literally about to jump off a bridge every night) is basically using timed check-ins once you put the baby down to sleep, patting or rubbing their back for twenty seconds, telling them you're there and that everything is okay...you get the idea. The first night it was every five minutes (which felt like hours), the next night seven minutes (which felt like days), the following night ten minutes (which felt like weeks), and finally fifteen minutes (which felt like an *I want to kill myself* eternity.)

There were times I had to leave the house and let Tay do the check-ins. It was brutal. My heart felt like it was breaking into a million little pieces with every cry. I hear this from many moms. It is not uncommon. But this felt different.

You see, when I was two, my amazing mother, who has always done everything to protect me and give me the world, accidentally traumatized me. Let me explain. In the eighties they were practicing the cry-it-out method—lock them in their room, they will eventually fall asleep, and when they wake up in the morning, they'll realize they can do it and ta-da! They can sleep in their own room. Everyone at her mommy-and-me class swore by it, the doctors supported it...it's just what people were doing at the time. So she tried it.

I have a vivid memory of being in the little area right by my childhood bedroom entrance, banging on the door, screaming and crying, *PLEASE LET ME OUT, MOMMY* until I eventually cried myself to sleep and passed out in that exact spot. I remember Mom shut the door, and I was left alone. Years later when this moment came up in therapy while discussing when I first felt abandoned, I called my mom to tell her about what we ended up uncovering in my session.

"Gabrielle," she said surprised on the other end of the phone. "You don't remember me sitting on the other side of the door talking to you the entire night? I *slept* on the other side of the door in case you woke up at all. I didn't leave the whole time."

Safe to say my two-year-old brain didn't remember that. I just remember feeling abandoned and alone.

Cut to me putting my five-and-a-half-month-old in his crib and leaving the room. I came back in to check on him as many times as he needed, which was usually only a few—but *BOY* was I triggered.

When I finally came to the realization that this was in fact a trigger and I was in fear of leaving the same trauma of being abandoned on my son, it all started to make sense.

He was an infant, not two years old, and I knew I was helping him create healthy sleep habits in a safe way. But it was damn near killing me because it was triggering me so deeply. After the first week, and wanting to throw in the towel, I sat in his rocking chair with him in the nursery after I finished nursing him. He was staring up at me, peacefully, and I said, "I understand the lesson you've been trying to get me to realize. I understand I have some more work to do around my abandonment fears. I got the message, thank you. Thank you for bringing it to my attention. I love you. You can go to sleep tonight."

I kid you not, Stone locked eyes with me and smiled. That night, I sang his song like I always did, put him in the crib, kissed him goodnight, and walked out of the room. I held my breath and braced myself for the crying.

It never came.

In fact, after that night there were very few nights of crying. He very quickly fell into being able to peacefully go to sleep. And me? I was able to reassess my fears of abandonment. This spawned many conversations with my husband and led to us growing even closer—partly because I was able to communicate my fears that were still present, and partly because Tay was able to truly see the little girl in me for the first time. It gave him a whole new understanding of why I get triggered and how he can be there to support me. I recognized the trigger, found out what it was about, and decided to acknowledge it—and what a gift was on the other side. Thank you for the first of many great lessons, my son.

When I was with my ex-husband, a lot of trauma took place that, at the time, I wasn't aware was happening to me. Daniel was obsessed with sex (which oddly enough, started *during* our relationship and was not something that had yet been awakened within him before). More often than I care to remember, I felt so pressured into having sex with him that I would just think to myself, *Well, might as well just lie here and get it over with*...and let it happen. As the relationship progressed, it wasn't just sex that was being asked of me. It was *Can you dress up in this very complicated lingerie that I bought you?* Or, *Will you dance for me while I throw $1 bills at you like a stripper?* And sometimes, *Say* *this, scream louder, do this position even if it hurts*, and *Act like the low-budget porn stars I've secretly been paying to watch online*. Okay, he didn't actually say the last one to me, but you get the point. What I didn't realize at the time, while I was lying there just to get it over with, was that I was actually disassociating. *My brain* was at a different place, often thinking of things I had to get done, career-related stuff on the horizon, or vacations I was excited about. *My body* was experiencing sex. Sex I didn't always want to be having. My body was experiencing trauma.

Years later when Tay and I had finally figured it out and were now living together in a home we bought, something really wild happened. Sorry in advance for the slightly graphic details. We had gone out for a fun dinner, had a few drinks, and came home to have sex. It ended up happening on our kitchen counter. While we were doing it, the condom we were using (because I had decided to get off birth control after God knows how many years) started to slip off. Tay and I had been in a committed relationship for a long time, having sex with and without protection when other birth control measures were in place. We knew that we were only active with each other, so the condom was because we were not yet ready to bring a child into the picture. When the condom started to slip off, he removed it and then, when the big shebang happened, he simply did what we normally did with no condom and pulled out. Once I realized this was what had happened, I had a full-blown fight-or-flight reaction. I, fucking, lost it.

I was instantly transported back to a time when Daniel had woken me up from a dead sleep by touching me to have sex. A time where I'd felt like my body was very much not my own. I had felt violated by it—and I experienced that same panic in that moment in the kitchen.

"YOU SHOULD HAVE TOLD ME," I screamed at Tay, who stood there, shocked and confused.

I collapsed onto the kitchen floor in tears. Even to me, this seemed like a strange reaction. I knew Tay loved me. I knew we were having consensual, very-much-wanted sex. But when that moment happened, it triggered me into the same feeling I'd had with my ex. Tay felt awful (although he did nothing wrong in the guidelines of our relationship), and we spent the rest of the night in bed, him comforting me, and us discussing what the hell had just taken place.

We ended up speaking to our therapist about the incident, and I was able to finally uncover a lot of the sexual trauma my first marriage had left with me. To this day, I feel guilty if Tay wants to have sex and I'm not in the mood. It is something I have to actively remind myself about—to honor the way I feel and not do things just because someone else might want to.

Our therapist suggested something really interesting that I want to share with you in case you were...yes...*triggered* when you read the words, *might as well just lie here and get it over with*. Because I have heard this statement from way too many friends, female podcast listeners, and women in general.

Why don't you just take sex off the table for a week or two? She made this suggestion so that we could take the pressure off of intimacy. It didn't have to lead to sex. The trauma that was stored in my body would always perk up when any make-outs or heavy petting would start, because I knew it was going to lead to having sex. Taking that finish line out of the equation meant that Tay and I could simply reconnect in an intimate way without the pressure of it all. And you know what? It actually made our sex life even better. We were suddenly able to really value that finish line when we got there, and I was able to relax and allow some of that trauma to be redefined inside of me.

Learning about this trigger and confronting it with my partner was monumental in our growth together and for me as an individual. Imagine how much extra trauma would have been experienced and stored up if I had continued to *just lie there and get it over with*. Besides the fact that my partner would have never wanted me to feel that way, what kind of a life is that? Sex and intimacy are meant to be enjoyed by—spoiler alert—both men and women. Working through this trigger has given me my power back not only in my sexuality but in my relationship with my body and my partner.

There have been some triggers in my relationship with Tay that have been subtle, and others where I actually had to laugh at the universe for putting something so blatantly obvious in my path.

I had come back from my grand healing adventure in Southeast Asia, woken up, and finally chosen to be with Tay. We had been in a happily-ever-after bubble for about five months and were getting ready to purchase our home together. To some, it is batshit crazy that we had been back and forth so many times and then just decided it was time to make one of the biggest financial commitments together—and that was not lost on me. The day before we were about to close escrow, I totally panicked. There I was, thirty-one years old, about to trade in my awesome little one-bedroom bungalow apartment, which was all mine, for a three-bedroom house that not only would come with a significant other and two dogs but also a seven-year-old child. That was a big life change. And suddenly, all my fear came boiling to the surface.

What if this doesn't work out?

What if I'm not a good step-parent?
What if we end up breaking up again?
What if, what if, WHAT IF?

At first, this might seem like a very normal and super-ficial reaction...but really, I was being triggered by a much deeper scenario.

It wasn't really about the financial commitment. It wasn't even really about the relationship commitment. What I ended up uncovering was so much more than all that. Subconsciously, what I was being plugged into was that good old fear of abandonment. *How is making a commitment like that plugging you into abandonment?* you might ask. Good question—lets dig in.

I was about to turn seven when my dad died. He was older than my mom. We were living in their happy dream home when it all happened. See where I'm going with this? I was moving into (at the time) our dream home with a man I loved, who happened to be more than a few years older than me—who also had a daughter who was the *exact age* I was when I lost my father. If that's not a mirror being held up for you to look at some shit, I don't know what is. So, at the core, I wasn't having a panic attack around buying a house—I was having a panic attack around *Tay is going to die on me like Dad died on Mom.*

I will never quite understand Tay's reaction to those emotions, but I will forever be grateful for it because it was a defining moment that not only saved but cemented our future. If their partner said she's totally panicking be-cause "what if it doesn't work out..." a day before escrow is closing on your first home together, 99% of men would probably say, "Holy shit, you have to be kidding me, I can't believe you're doing this to me...*again.*" But instead, Tay gently grabbed my face, looked deep into my eyes, and said,

"Look. Either this is all going to work out and we're going to be totally happy and in love—or it doesn't, and we end up friends and business partners. Either way it's a smart investment." I mean...WHERE DID I FIND THIS MAN? It is not lost on me *now* that, in this moment, I was in turn triggering one of his fears from his first marriage. The back-and-forth, the questioning of commitment, it was all being thrown in his face for *him* to heal.

Working through these triggers both individually and together has helped us recognize when they're happening. Suddenly, if a fight happens, it's not just, *Why are you being such an asshole right now?* Instead, we think, *Oh, this is a reaction because you're triggered.* Some of the most valuable information you can have about your partner is what their triggers are and what plugs them into said triggers. It allows you to have a completely different reaction and also to help heal that pain point together.

This trigger has been a recurring one for me in our relationship—and it has been showing up dancing like a fucking showgirl and throwing confetti since our son was born. I constantly have to stay on top of my intrusive thoughts about death. Specifically, Tay's death. I wrote the chapter about losing my dad the same week that Tay's back went out. It was one of the scariest times in our relationship. Stone was only a few weeks old, and Tay woke me up in the middle of the night, completely paralyzed in pain and unable to move. There I was, at 5 a.m., with a two-hundred-and-fifteen-pound husband I was not able to physically move and a newborn who was about to wake up any second and need me. I felt pressure. I felt panic. I felt helpless. Boom. *Trigger.* What if I am creating the same exact pattern I watched my mom live through? What if my son ends up losing his dad the way I did and then I have to raise him on my own? What if I have to be strong through all of that—*again*. Now...is it possible? Sure. It's also possible that I walk outside tomorrow morning and get trampled by a rainbow unicorn at thirty-six. What is more likely in this scenario is that I ended up creating this weirdly similar path to what my mother walked through *so that I could rewrite it and create it differently*. And what a fucking gift that will be, not only for my child but for little seven-year-old Gabrielle who just wanted everything to be okay.

I feel as if I need to take this moment, in this chapter, to point out something huge that I have come to know recently after working through some of these triggers and healing. I really did have a realization after my Europe trip when I discovered: *I am never truly abandoned because I will never abandon myself.* So while I do know in my heart that I am rewriting this story and that Tay and I will have many amazing years together, I also know that, no matter what, I will be okay. I have survived it before, and I will survive it again. There might be pain, struggles, and challenges...*but I will eventually be okay.*

When Tay handled that situation the way he did before we bought our home, something shifted for me. And while that death trigger still rears its ugly head from time to time, it feels different now. There has been a weird sort of acceptance—that no matter what the outcome ends up being, I will be okay, and I've found some peace in that. Another small piece of letting go of the control I've always so desperately held onto since I was a little girl. It was then, after getting through that moment with him, that I felt the last little bit of my resistance fall away, and I was able to fully and completely commit to him, the relationship, the step-kid, the life. And now, here we are.

Relationships are mirrors.
Mirrors show you triggers.
Choose to heal.

Taymour

Since Gabs explained what triggers are and how they work, I will just dive in. Head first. I have three lovely little triggers that I will discuss in detail to better illustrate just how fucked up I truly am. Just kidding.

As shitty as triggers can be and the potential harm they can cause you, they also serve as a platform you can stand on and, if done correctly, from which you can jump off to make a change. They are the doorways to our hindrances. If you choose to open those doors and make a change in yourself, those triggers eventually fade away. But as sure as those healed triggers will fade away, rest assured, new ones will emerge. So it is better to find a way to address rather than ignore.

They will find you in loneliness and in relationships alike, and they won't go away until you get to the root of them. That's the thing about triggers...*they only grow stronger when ignored*. Sometimes, I refer to my triggers as that little voice in my head. They are always speaking to me, DAMN IT, but they aren't always saying the right things. Triggers can be a serious deal breaker in life if you can't figure them out.

Time to lay my trigger cards on the table for you all. In no particular order, they are, abandonment, the fear of leaving too soon, and disrespect.

My mother's death caused a hundred and one triggers in me. The loss was so powerful that I felt abandoned, which triggered an emotion in me that I desperately wanted to numb. I numbed it until I finally learned the reasons I was numbing it.

Secondly, and somewhat related to my mother's passing and abandonment, is my fear of leaving my kids too soon. I'm no longer the young dad that I wanted to be when I was a kid. That combined with having a parent leave me too soon leaves my door to triggerville wide open.

And lastly, but by no means least-ly, are my triggers around disrespect. All three of these triggers poke their heads into my world now and again, some more often, and more severely, than others.

You don't have to be Freud to assess that my abandonment issue stemmed from my mother's death. It's rather obvious. Death in a young person's life leaves an indelible and often unexplainable void in their existence. It certainly did in mine. From the very moment my mom went down, I felt lost. I had fallen deep into a black hole, the biggest fucking void in existence. Cue the triggered reaction. I searched and searched for anything to either take the pain away or replace it. Anything to fill that void. Being a serial monogamist filled the void. Getting into fights filled that void. Numbing all of it with substances filled that void. Even being a parent filled that void. But it was all simply momentary—and that quick fix would inevitably fade.

I really needed to stop and assess once and for all. I went back to the drawing board, back to therapy, to see if I could unearth something from my inner child. It wasn't until after two separate yet wonderful conversations with two of the most influential women in my life, my aunt, Mama Goose, and my mother-in-law, Dee Wallace, that I came to learn something powerful: *I don't need to fill the void.*

The void will always be there. It is how I choose to view it that makes the difference. That struck me rather curious. A light bulb went off in my head. You see, when you bear witness to death, you develop a relationship to it. You know it will always be there. Because I knew it to be inevitable and rather ruthless at times, I have always respected death. But was there a way I could respect the abandonment void just the same?

Yes. I could respect it by accepting it. It was simply a choice I (and the little thirteen-year-old inside of me who lost his mom) had to decide to make. To finally move on with my life and not allow that abandonment void to define me—*just as my mother would want me to do.*

It certainly helped to have Gabrielle in my corner. I credit her with a lot of my growth and change. She has always seen the power in me. She encourages me and cheers me on. My mother did the same, and I was left yearning and searching for that when she died. I can see it in Gabrielle's eyes when she looks at me. It is the exact same way my mom used to look at me.

When I finally realized I could respect and honor that void, sit in it, and not be consumed with trying to fill it...it all fell into place. I was no longer living in fear that Gabrielle, or those feelings of warmth and love I had experienced with my mom, would leave me. I could finally accept what was in front of me. I could breathe. It has been a few years now since I have been triggered by abandonment. I know part of that is me growing through it, but a big part of it is Gabrielle understanding it and holding space in her heart for it—as I do for her. She regularly checks in with me when she senses I may be feeling off. And vice versa. It is exactly what a good communicative relationship needs. We came together with such a similar abandonment trauma; it was the perfect recipe for either intense disaster or immense healing. Because we recognized those triggers and helped each other feel safe with them...here we are.

Truth be told, I am normally not a sad person, nor do I really suffer bouts of heavy depression, but the thought of dying and not being here for my children triggers me toward a fear-based mindset that is undeniable. I get so sad it borders on depression and it can become unrelenting. I think most parents feel some level of what I am talking about.

For as long as I can remember, I have always thought I would die young. Having a mother die of an unexpected aneurysm at a young age would inevitably cause such a thought. It was in my cards and in my makeup. Now that I am fifty, I have surpassed *young*. I have legitimately entered *old* or *late middle-aged*. Whatever the hell that means. But that thought lingers. I go to the doctor, they assure me I'm fine, that it isn't really something they can fully predict, and blah blah blah. None of it matters. My trauma brain convinces itself that I am for sure dying of a massive aneurysm and will be found in the side yard by one of my kids, just as I found my mother. Luckily, now that I've surpassed the age my mother left me at, that fear has begun to subside a little.

This is a trigger. Like the others, I had to get to the root of it. In this case, it's rather elementary. My mother died unexpectedly young, which triggered a slew of emotions, including a debilitating fear of leaving my children. To not get completely engulfed by those emotions, I actively remind myself to live for each day and not look too far into the future. Pay attention to the moment in front of you. Live healthy and desire longevity but don't let it get in the way of your dance. Together, Gabs and I have created our own philosophy that reflects these morals. Because we both lost a parent, we have been actively fending off triggers left and right like freaking sword fighters. Instead of letting it take us deep down the dark rabbit hole, we just chalk it up to having a little "trauma brain" and move on. Let the moment pass and not go into that dark hole. Stay on top of your thoughts. *Focus on what you want.* When you do that enough times, the cycle has no choice but to break. And eventually, it fades into the past.

This chapter turned out to be the most difficult to write. In the beginning, when Gabs and I decided what to write about, I thought the divorce chapter would be my tank of snakes from *Pee-wee's Big Adventure*. I thought writing this chapter would be a breeze, but I realized that it isn't all that easy to write about the things you don't like to talk about. As you unearth yourself, so to speak, you make discoveries that can be uncomfortable. It is painful to open up the wounds that have created triggers in us. And this last trigger is the hardest one to dive into. It is the one that I'm most ashamed of. The one that is most detrimental to me and my loved ones. I'd like to call it the silent rage...only it's not that silent once the rage part hits. Some people like to call it a temper. Others call it anger. A lack of control. Let's open up the wound together, shall we?

I come from a long line of Persian hotheads and Irish/Welsh ruffians. We like to drink. We like to fight. We like to love. And we do it all to the utmost. I've been in more fights in my life than there are fingers and toes on everyone in my entire family. And I'm not proud of that. I used to love to shake it up, and I was always in the middle of it. Looking back on it all now, it is rather embarrassing. It was fun and scary at the time, but fully juvenile and pointless. As I get older and start living more existentially, I can't help but think what a waste of our time on earth it is beating one another up. I wish I could tell myself that very thing when the spirit moves me in that direction.

I'm sure some of the men reading this book are able to relate to these same impulses. I think the generations past raised their young men with different ideas of what it means to be "a man," and it is rather hard to break some of those molds. My hope in writing this book is for other men to see there is strength in vulnerability, courage in healing, and pride with accountability. That, to me, is the very definition of being a good man—and I hope that this chapter can help break some of those old ideas.

I have an impulse control issue, and I'm here to claim it. There are times when I can't control my emotions and subsequently my actions. Gross. It's embarrassing to write it, but here I am standing atop the mountain shouting it to all of you. As I get older, and continually work on it, I harness just a little more control each and every day—but I'm an imperfect work in progress. I am human and still have incidents here and there. Those incidents don't always lead to a physical confrontation, but they stem from the same place. Lack of impulse control. For the longest time I just chalked it up to liking to fight, or being hotheaded, but there was something deep-seated that I was not seeing. Something at the root. I was getting triggered.

Two such incidents, at opposite ends of the spectrum yet stemming from the same trigger, will better illustrate where it comes from inside of me. One thing I have always placed great importance on is respect. Respect for your parents, respect for women, respect for the elderly, respect for people in general. My father was and still is a wonderfully respectful gentleman and always treats people with kindness and respect. Both my father and mother instilled in me from a young age that we treat everyone with the same respect. Simple concept.

Well, when someone shows a lack of respect, I lose it. Or I should say, *it triggers me*. In a big way—and then I lose it.

Take for instance my loving daughter. Juni is very respectful *most* of the time. On the occasions she is not, we attribute it up to her being an angsty pre-teen. There are times I have raised my voice too high or walked away or said something I later wished I could take back. Don't get me wrong, there are times when I just want to grab her and scream, "WHAT ARE YOU THINKING?" But I think that has been said by every single parent on the planet. The bottom line is that I get close. I let my temper get the best of me in some of those delicate times, and I always end up regretting it. Let me be clear, I have never hit or spanked my child—EVER. But I can be scary at times and use fear as a tactic, and I am realizing that there is just no space for that. But *why* do I do it? To prove my point? To prove that I am right? Where is that stemming from? It can't just be based on respect or the lack thereof. I was being triggered from a deep emotional place that I couldn't put my finger on.

Then, one night, something interesting happened. Gabs and I went to see a movie. I believe it was the new Batman, so it was completely sold out. We got there rather early and witnessed about eight young guys getting rowdy before the movie had begun. We settled in, but I kept my side-eye on these guys. I don't know what it was, but I knew they were trouble. I could feel it. Finally, the movie started, and I know that everyone in that theater that night hoped they would just shut up. No dice. They continued until someone went and got management. They were in our row, so they needed to pass us to get out. As they approached us to pass and exit, one of them turned to the woman sitting next to Gabrielle, leaned into her face, and called her "a fucking bitch."

That was it for me. I saw red. I kicked his leg so that he would trip, and the second he got up, I had my hands around his collar. I was so triggered, I about blacked out. I pushed him along, and he and his friends began threatening me. But it was easy for them to see that they had messed with the wrong bull, and they left the theater. Poor Gabrielle was in fear the whole rest of the movie after what happened. Once the movie finished, neither of us able to tell you if Robert Pattinson was a good Batman or not, we headed home to a very in-depth conversation about what the hell had taken over me. I honestly didn't have an answer for her. It was probably the first time in my life I didn't have an answer for something. I really didn't know what to say. I compared it to the feeling I got when Juni would push the envelope of disrespect, which seemed to stem from the same place.

At that moment, I knew I had to go deeper. I knew there was something tangible there that I just couldn't see. I called my therapist the next day. What we got to was mind blowing and it uncovered something deep within me.

As a young boy I witnessed many arguments and fights between my parents that sent me into fight-or-flight mode. As you read in Gabrielle's section, it is that descent into fight-or-flight thinking that creates the trigger. Witnessing or being on the receiving end of disrespect is a trigger for me—I associate it with what I witnessed growing up, and I immediately default to that fight-or-flight feeling. My inner child has been inside me, all this time, not knowing how to get out of that fight-or-flight panic. Whether it was one of my parents disrespecting the other, or witnessing one of their grand altercations, I was too young to understand. All I understood in those moments was yelling and fighting. As a boy, I would do anything in my power to stop it, but my power was not enough. Now that I am older, my power *is* enough. Enough to use fear as a tactic. Enough to have the potential to come out in scary ways. Now it is about harnessing that power. Realizing that there is a trigger inside and figuring out how to manage the emotion that trigger causes. After working on it in therapy, I have become able to harness the beast and react differently. To choose to not be triggered when Juni acts out. To choose to not see red when I witness blatant disrespect in a movie theater.

It all works when you put in the work. Regarding that other side, that itch to shake it up or that insatiable need to be right or prove someone else wrong...look, I'm getting older, growing tired. I really believe in the existential answer to life—zoom out. We are just on a big freaking rock floating through space and our time here is short. Rather than wasting your time proving something right or someone wrong, relish the short time you are here by loving one another and letting them have their own beliefs. It is not up to you to correct them if they don't fall in line with yours. You don't have to love them; you just have to let them be— and I am still constantly working on that.

During one of my therapy sessions, my angel of a therapist said the most profound thing to me. She ever so eloquently quoted the most beautiful passage from a poem I had ever heard. It was the quote from Rumi that I mentioned in the Friendships chapter, and it entered me and sank directly to the bottom of my heart. My soul and spirit sucked it right up, and it was locked away inside me forever. I say it to myself a thousand and one times a day. A mantra, if you will. A slogan to myself, that guides my way and acts as a constant reminder. Not just for this particular trigger, but for life and every obstacle that comes my way. And so, it rings...

> "Out beyond the ideas of wrongdoing
> and rightdoing,there is a field.
> I will meet you there."
> —Rumi

I'm proud to say that, as I have gotten older, I have started to look deep within myself rather than just existing. I'm taking accountability for my presence and, in doing so, learning about myself and my triggers. The things that motivate me versus the things that discourage me. You have to know the things that make you tick. If you blindly walk through life not understanding how and why you do things, then you are simply asking for a dull life on a one-way street, with nobody traveling with you...and we like companions.

I believe our similar triggers are a cosmic connection between Gabrielle and me. I like to think that the universe brought us together because of them. So we can help one another during those times. But that's the romantic in me.

Make no mistake about it, Gabrielle and I have made space for each other's triggers since the beginning of our time. We have developed a healthy, gentle way of navigating our way through it, all while holding each other's hands as we continue to grow and new triggers show up. It's the whole "till death do us part" stuff from the wedding. You remember? But really, it is the quintessential ingredient to making a relationship grow, heal, deepen, and last. To be able to make space for your partner, trauma brain or not. To experience life as it comes, allowing it to affect them, letting it trigger them, and still be there to hold them, regardless of how it makes you feel. That is the partnership we all yearn for. That is what I have found through healing my triggers. And it is my greatest shining star.

Losing Your Way

"If you don't get lost, there's a chance you may never be found."
— Anonymous

Gabrielle

This chapter was a last-minute addition to the book. Not because we needed more content or felt like the book wasn't complete—but because during the course of this editing process, Tay and I both experienced something quite uncomfortable. It's something many people shy away from sharing for a myriad of reasons—to protect their image, to keep themselves safe and comfortable, or even because they simply do not want to admit it to themselves. And after experiencing it so freshly, I knew it was something we needed to include for you all to read. How do I explain what happened in the simplest way possible?

We lost our way.

No need to panic at the disco. I don't mean we almost broke up or that he almost hopped into bed with a barely legal Instagram model. I simply mean that we both, as individuals, were faced with some new challenges and old traumas that came to the surface to be healed. Things that, while good in the long run, suck a big fat dick while you're in them...excuse my French.

I've battled with imposter syndrome on and off since I stepped into my career as an author. I don't think it was until I was well into writing my second book and *Eat, Pray, #FML* had hit best-seller multiple times that I even uttered the words "I'm an author." Even now, after two books, a podcast with hundreds of episodes, and enough messages from readers to fill the pages of its own book, I still sometimes hear a little voice that quietly asks...*what are you even doing in this world?*

I have always promised my readers, listeners, and followers authenticity. If I'm having the time of my life, I'll share that happiness. If I'm at Café Misery, table for one, I'll let you know the time and date of my pity party. With so much fake happiness and toxic comparisons on social media, I have vowed to always be real and honest—*because it's okay not to be okay.* So when my mental health decided to take a balletic swan dive into the deep end, I looked at Tay, sighed, and said, "Shit. I guess we have to write about this."

I will never forget a well-known friend who called me before the release of a book she had written with her then husband. She was miserable. She was questioning everything between the two of them, including whether she was going to stay in the relationship. When I asked her why she was allowing her unhappiness to continue in her marriage, she said something that has always stuck with me.

I can't leave. We're about to release our book. It will ruin everything.

Thinking about that particular conversation and that particular relationship has haunted me throughout this writing process. It stoked my imposter syndrome whenever it sparked. How was I supposed to release this book about healing yourself and doing the work if I was drowning in my own sea of healing? Who was I to teach these lessons? Well, the answer I arrived at was something I already knew deep down, but even for Tay and me, it bears repeating:

Just because you lose your way does not mean you are forever lost.

It's just another layer to your healing. This too shall pass.

It's okay not to be okay.

After Tay and I welcomed our son, Stone, into the world, I was determined I was going to do motherhood like I do everything else—really freaking well. Yes, my type-A self was sure I could control everything, sidestep any post-partum depression, juggle all the things (while doing a little twirl), and rock the shit out of being a new mom. (If you're a mother yourself, you're probably laughing right about now.) And this was all despite the fact that we had just tackled the three biggest stressors in life—buying a house, getting married, and having a baby—all within a six-month period. We had checked them all off the list pretty flawlessly. And for the first month after Stone was born, I was gracefully pulling it off. Motherhood was going great. Then everything around me began to collapse one by one.

We were hit with a difficult financial blow we weren't expecting when Tay's industry went on strike. He had a falling out with a family member that caused a significant amount of emotional stress and grief. My stepdad was diagnosed with cancer out of nowhere, which flared up every *Daddy's gonna die* wound I have in me. Jess and I had our first massive falling out and stopped speaking. And my two-hundred-and-fifteen pound husband's back went out, twice, resulting in a 5 a.m. ambulance call and a very helpless me praying my newborn wouldn't wake up right then.

Suddenly, I wasn't only not rocking motherhood, I wasn't rocking life. I was so angry and so frustrated that all of this was happening *now*. I often still look back and wish

I could have experienced those first few months without all of the outside catastrophes, because I feel like I would have actually been...pretty okay.

I had been worried about postpartum depression a lot during my pregnancy. The amount of fear spread about it on social media was clearly targeting my subconscious...and my algorithm. I've also struggled with adrenal deficiency, like my mother, which when not addressed, can present in a very similar way to postpartum depression.

There I was, trying to keep up the façade (honestly, mostly for my own psyche) that I was rocking this phase of life, when on the inside, I was completely drowning. Drowning and trying to patch the holes being poked in the little boat I was in. Drowning and trying to keep everyone around me afloat.

It wasn't something you could see from the outside because, most of the time, I was pretty fine. It was only when I got hit with something, or a fight happened, or I got completely overstimulated, that I would recognize that something really wasn't right. It would cause a downward spiral that I was completely and utterly unable to pull out of. The only way I can really describe it is like this: In the Robin Williams movie *What Dreams May Come,* his beloved wife takes her own life. When he gets to heaven, excited to reunite with her, he quickly realizes that she ended up somewhere else because of the way she passed. He goes on a quest to find her that takes him through dark and treacherous areas made of things you see in nightmares. When he finally finds her, she is trapped in her own personal hell. It is their home, but abandoned, run down, and falling apart. It is dark. It is cold. It is the perfect representation of what things look like through the frightening gray lens of depression. No matter how hard she tried, she could not get out of the house. That is how the spiral feels. You *consciously* know it's temporary. You *consciously* know things aren't that awful. But your consciousness is no longer there to hold your hand and guide your way. Instead, you are simply stuck, trapped inside yourself, wondering where the light went.

As I write this, it has been sixteen months since I gave birth. While these spirals are now fewer and farther between, recent pressures and changes have led them to not so gently let me know they are still very much there. At times it has made me feel out of control. Other times it has made me feel absolutely insane. I do not envy anyone having to experience this in their life.

You can imagine how difficult it is to have healthy communication during one of these spirals. There have been many times when Tay has had to just allow me to win in fear of what might come if he kept defending his side. It has aided my imposter syndrome in its random attacks on my spirit. Who am I to be helping others on their healing journey if I am fighting for my sanity in the depths of my own hellish spiral?

Then, one day, I remembered something I have said in many different interviews when asked what advice I have for anyone going through a difficult time: *No matter how dark it might seem right now, the light at the end of the tunnel is more beautiful than you could ever imagine. Keep going.*

Keep going. It's really that simple. It's what I've always done. You keep going. When Daddy dies? Keep going. When you find out your ex-husband is cheating, keep going. When you get heartbroken by the man who love bombed you? Keep going. When you're scared to publish the book? Quit the job? Take the trip? Look within? Do the work? *Keep, fucking, going.*

The year-and-a-half long process of writing this book and the recent challenges Tay and I have faced together have only brought more lessons. I have seen that, even when rocked by emotional earthquakes, my marriage can hold strong on the foundation we've built. The biggest gift of all is knowing that, even in my darkest spirals, I would rather be doing it all with my husband as opposed to anyone else. My people have stepped up, supported, and loved me through it all. And even when things felt scary and out of control, I showed up for myself. What a beautiful reminder that I will never, ever abandon myself—even when things collapse around me or hormones and depression break down my door.

The stories in this book are simply a compilation of our truths, shared and individual experiences, and what those experiences have helped us learn. We are so very far from perfect—although I can confidently say this is the happiest and healthiest relationship I have ever been in. Does that mean we don't go through hard times? Or have disagreements? Or experience imposter syndrome? No. It simply means we have done the work in the past and, most importantly, continue to do the work when it arrives anew. There are days you will feel as if you can climb mountains and conquer the world—and days where you will wonder why the world suddenly seems so devastatingly dark. Both are okay. Both are part of being human. The only job we all really have is to just keep going.

Taymour

I'm not going to lie—just yesterday I wanted to stop writing and not even entertain the idea of finishing this book, let alone publishing it. There have been quite a few times in the process of writing that I have spiraled and wanted to throw in the towel. It is an uncomfortable place to be, let me tell you. Why? Simple. How can I rightly explain to you, our readers, just how glorious life can be if you *choose yourself* or *love yourself* or realize that *you are enough* when I am continually faced with moments that challenge those very ideas in my own life? It would be unfair to you to just show you how good things can be when you have it all figured out—so I won't do that. Instead of bailing on this whole book idea, I will instead explain—and beg of you to listen—that life is a continual work in progress.

All the lessons you think you have learned will change over time, and you will be faced with some of the same situations you've met in the past. Or new situations will present themselves for new lessons to be learned. It can be cyclically maddening if you let it be, or it can be positively glorious if you trust the path. Realize that this journey will encompass the good, the bad, and the ugly. Life ebbs and flows, there are peaks and valleys, death, new life, and all the other things we spoke of in this book. Find a way, deep in your heart, to realize, accept, and inevitably love all aspects of life, even if they aren't fun while they are happening. Life's ups and downs won't change, and I've come to the conclusion that the only thing that *can* change in the equation is my perspective. But prior to coming to that conclusion, I fought long and hard with my own insecurities revolving around self-worth and abandonment, which continually peek around the corner in times of trial. Just when you thought you had moved past those dark feelings, they are there to say, "Hello, hello, it's me again."

I have always been a heart-on-the-sleeve type of guy. If I am in a down mood, you will know it. Yes, I can act happy in those times if needed, but with me you usually get my genuine self, and it certainly isn't always smiles and laughter. The best way to illustrate this is to explain how wildly intense the last year of my life has been.

The year 2023 laid the groundwork for serious reflection on all of my previous lessons and then some. My life seemed to be a revolving door of massive events, some good, some bad. It was the year my son was born, so it was one of the more pivotal and memorable years in my life, but it certainly came with its fair share of tribulations, most of which I am still filing away slowly. Let's start with my union going on strike. I am a proud member of the Screen Actors Guild and have been for two decades. I support my union fully and wholeheartedly, but as a professional working actor and teacher, my sole income relies on the industry in motion. So when we hit the picket lines, I, and 95% of the actors in this industry, went from hero to zero. I literally went from making enough money to afford my share of the big new house we'd bought to earning not one dollar. It was a very scary time. On top of that, I was then burdened with a severe back crisis related to the stress of not being able to provide. And in rushed the first of many massive surges of the dreaded *I am not enough* feelings.

You can see where this is going, right? Around every corner, there were more of those feelings, almost as if they fed off each other. The more I entertained the idea of not being enough, the more it seemed to manifest into my reality. Eventually, my back began to heal and our industry revved up again, and those feelings began to subside, but I didn't diligently handle them when I should have. No, no, they were there, resting, waiting until I was most vulnerable, which incidentally happened to be a few days ago, in the middle of writing this book. Hence the addition of this chapter. Coincidence? I don't think so.

Change is never easy, and Gabs and I are going through some pretty heavy change. We are in the process of selling our home and renovating and relocating to Gabrielle's childhood home. This was always the eventual game plan, but it happened a lot sooner than any of us were planning. This is where my insecurities reintroduced themselves. This plan was set into motion to relieve the immense financial pressure we were experiencing. A lot of that pressure was caused by me not being able to work and then being somewhat complacent when work started coming back in. And that is a hard pill to swallow for me. I became comfortable in staying home with my family and taking work when it came rather than going out and looking for it. But that was a problem because I just wasn't bringing in enough. We are and always have been a two-income household. At the beginning I was making more, having booked a fairly large commercial campaign, but when Gabs launched her books, she was the clear breadwinner for a time. Look, I am not old-fashioned in any way. I totally believe that women should make as much as men, and it doesn't matter who in the family makes the money as long as everyone is happy. I feel like our society equates the ability to provide financially with being "a good man." While I disagree with that, it has been instilled in many men, including me, which makes anything less than that feel difficult to accept. I want to be able to provide equally, and I want my family to be able to rely on me at every turn. When I can't, or they don't, I am left with the familiar yet painful feeling of *I am not enough*. When Gabs would approach me with valid concerns, I would get defensive and angry. So off to therapy we went.

Now, here is the thing about therapy. I don't just go to make my partner happy, I actually go to find solutions. That makes a big difference. Don't just go because your partner wants you to. Don't do it for them. Do it for the relationship. Try to understand yourself just a little more. There are actual solutions to the problems we experience, so have an open mind, really try to understand the root cause of your problems, and find a solution. Plus, there is nothing better than an outside perspective.

In therapy, Gabs and I have one stark rule and that is that we will be completely honest. In one session, I was honest about feeling like I was climbing a hill of stress. I felt like I was not enough. I felt criticized and blamed, but I knew it was justified, which made it far worse. Because of those feelings, I began to feel abandoned. And once that happens, all hell breaks loose inside of me. I start acting out. I make rash decisions. I get upset at the littlest things. But you know what? Just giving those feelings a voice suddenly made the gray storm clouds part. Although it is difficult at times to admit your wrongdoings and take accountability, the more you do so, the easier life becomes. To acknowledge that we make mistakes and try to learn from those mistakes is about as evolved as one can get.

Lessons will come and go for all of eternity. It's just the way life is, so accept it or continue to live under a dark cloud of boring existence. An existence shrouded in monotony with very little growth or change. As difficult as the past year has been, culminating with this last week of panic and self-doubt, I am so fortunate that I have a partner that sticks with me. Together we help each other through each lesson. Walking away from therapy and really digesting what we have been through this past year, I can begin to visualize my next steps. We came to so many realizations in the one session, but three glaring lessons presented themselves that I am forever grateful for.

It was the first time in our relationship that I didn't feel heard, and I learned that sometimes that is all you need, regardless of whether you are right or wrong. It also very strategically brought to light old patterns of mine that I am not proud of. Complacency and comfort have always been key ingredients to my occasional lack of ambition. Now that I have acknowledged that, I am able to work on breaking those habits. It allowed Gabs and I to see where minor cracks had appeared from the sometimes daunting pressures of life so that we can begin to fill them one at a time, together, reinforcing our foundation. But most of all, it gave me the opportunity to prove to myself that *I am enough* just as I am. Money, relationships, children—none of that makes up your DNA. You and you alone make it up, and once you stand true in that discovery, your life will begin to flourish.

No one has it all figured out. We are all just going through this life trying to ease our path by any means necessary. In all of our pursuits there will be ups and downs and lessons flying at us at the speed of light. We all need to acknowledge and accept that it is totally okay to not always be okay. Only then will we stop measuring our worth by society's standards and realize our only purpose in this life is to grow and be happy. We are never really done learning and growing—and I'll learn this lesson fifty more times if it means reaching the happiness I know this life can offer.

Our Relationship Journey

"Remember the rivers and how they merged our hearts, never apart."
– Trevor Hall

Gabrielle

If you haven't read *The Ridiculous Misadventures of a Single Girl*, then you don't know that it took Tay and me (and by that I really mean me) a while to figure it the fuck out. There was back and forth. Breakups and make-ups. Four times to be exact. Other people. Drama. But there was one thing that stayed constant throughout it all—our love and respect for each other.

I actually can't wait to read his section of this book—because those of you that *have* read *The Ridiculous Misadventures* obviously have never gotten to hear his perspective of it all...until now.

There's a lot of dangerous information out there about soulmates, twin flames, and excuses that will 100% make you think that your toxic roller-coaster relationship is *for sure* meant to be. I am here to tell you that 99.9% of the time, that is not the case. They don't really love you, they're not going to change, and the fact that he hearted your five-paragraph text message was in fact *not* a response—it is bullshit.

What *is* valid and what *more* people should be talking about on whatever the newest app is on social media this week is that relationships are *mirrors*. Every relationship, whether it be a significant other, family member, work colleague, or friend...*you attracted into your life for a reason.*

Before digging into my relationship journey with Tay, I want to touch on this in a broader way for a moment—because it is so life-changingly important. Ready for the bombshell? The asshole who broke your heart, the narcissists who keep seeking you out, the cheaters who keep lying to you, and even the good ones who are just missing something...*YOU CREATED THEM ALL.*

What? Gabrielle, I would never *choose* to be in a horrible relationship like that. I would never *attract* people who would hurt me. I would never *create* failed relationship after failed relationship. Are you feeling triggered? Did you get that out of your system there? Good. Now, *yes the fuck you did.*

Does this mean you deserve any of that? Absolutely not. It doesn't mean you are a terrible person whose karma says *you deserve to be cheated on*. But if there is a pattern in your life, best believe you are subconsciously attracting that for a reason. It is your choice if you want to recognize it, take accountability for it, and heal it—or, by all means, continue attracting the same pieces of shit who have been wrecking your heart. We always have a choice.

My relationship history is a prime example of this. When my father died, my little six-year-old-self created a subconscious belief. *When I love someone, they die.* In more practical terms, fear of abandonment. That belief was then firmly reinforced when Josh passed away in the car accident. I was walking around in life knowing deep in my soul that the men in my life were going to abandon me. Was this conscious? Of course not. It's our SUBconscious that attracts things into our lives so our brain can then go, *"Look, look! See! I told you! They all abandon me!"*

First, I attracted Daniel—who abandoned me in many ways. First, in a physical sense, choosing to disrespect my body. He abandoned the vows he made to me on our wedding day. He abandoned me with every lie he told. And the universe said, "Okay, Gabrielle, are you ready to heal this now?" And I said, "No thank you, universe, I'll take door number two instead."

Behind door number two was an (unbeknownst to me) unhealed Latin lover named Javier. I imagine the universe laughing and saying, "Jesus, she didn't get the message with the cheating and the divorce...how can we make this more literal for her? OH! Let's have him *literally* abandon her days before getting on a plane to a trip HE invites her on. Brilliant."

You see, because I had the subconscious belief that men were going to abandon me, I was continuously attracting just that—so my brain could then be proven right. How exhausting, no? That time, thankfully, I got the message loud and clear.

I went, healed, loved myself, healed some more...and most importantly, took accountability for the fact that I had been attracting those people to learn this lesson and heal this belief that had been running my life since I was a little girl. I stepped out of the victimhood of *why does this keep happening to me* and stepped into the power of *I'm ready to attract something different now, thank you very much.* Once I did that, who did I end up attracting? Someone who would never abandon me—Tay. But that's not to say that relationship didn't come with its own challenges and mirrors.

I'll never forget the first time Tay and I hung out in 2019. We had met almost a decade earlier on a film shoot. We totally connected on a soul level but were both in respective relationships and it was never a romantic feeling—

it was just a soul connection. Over the years, we had messaged on Facebook—congrats on this life event, how are you doing, all the typical social media relationship check-ins. But after running into him at my favorite bar and finding out that he, too, was in the divorced-and-floundering club, we decided to grab dinner.

When I tell you I didn't think it was a date, I mean that very seriously. I showed up in leggings, with no makeup on, and proceeded to word vomit about both my exes and tell him I was still very much in love with the latest one. Apparently, that was not a red flag to my now husband but a sign that we were obviously destined to be together. Hey, I never said he didn't have some toxic shit to work out when we first met.

However, it wasn't until a night after too much partying, when I ended up sleeping at his house (and, for lack of other places, in his bed), that I realized this man was...different. Why? Very simple. He didn't try to have sex with me.

If you want the details of our love story and how we made it (some might say barely or by the grace of God), I'll let you dive into my second book. Actually, if you've ever questioned how strong our relationship is, read that book and imagine Tay sitting in our home, reading the rough draft in one sitting—you'll quickly know what an incredible man he is. What I want to focus on here, in this book, are the main things that showed up in our relationship mirror. And let me assure you, facing your shit in the mirror is a messy, complicated bitch of a job.

I'm not the only one who deals with abandonment in the depths of my DNA. The fact that Tay and I share such an oddly specific trauma is not lost on us. We both, in our childhoods, not only lost a parent but were the one to discover them. I lost my father, instilling the fear of abandonment with *men*, and he lost his mother, creating the fear of abandonment with *women*. So, is it really a surprise these two people ended up together to have the opportunity to heal this lifelong fear?

I think Tay has always dived headfirst into relationships when he sees potential with someone. His friends used to joke that every "one" was "the one." And I think a lot of that started after his mother died. Unconsciously, I think he was trying to do exactly what I was doing with the men in my life—fill the void the parent left. Because subconsciously, if he didn't have Mom, he wasn't safe. He wasn't enough. He used relationships to fill the void left by his mom, so if he didn't have a relationship, he wasn't okay. He went from one relationship to another as a serial monogamist. Until he met me, who, because of what a mess my life was at the time, threw his biggest fear directly in his face...*four times*.

For a very long time I deeply blamed myself for that and felt immense guilt. How could I have triggered the deepest wound of the person who never came close to touching mine? How horrible am I for going back and forth and allowing this man to wait and hope and guess while I figured my shit out? Then one day, in a conversation with (who else) my mother, she (as she always does) pointed out something that completely changed my perspective in the most freeing way.

"Gabrielle. You always talk about why *you* attracted *Tay* into your life. It's not all about you, you know." *GASP*. Excuse me, Mother, how could you say such a thing? Kidding, obviously. "Tay obviously attracted you, as you were during that time in your life, to learn lessons of his own." When I sat down to talk with Tay about it, a huge weight was lifted off my shoulders. The experience that we went through, me being in and out and, in its triggered form, abandoning him...was exactly what *he* needed to heal. He needed to know that *he was enough* without a relationship—and I was giving him the perfect mirror to force himself to look at that.

The healing on my end was a little more obvious...now that I see it, at least. I had finally attracted someone who was never going to abandon me, someone who was different from all the ones who had come before, to play out that same tired scenario in different ways. Now the obstacle was finally allowing myself to accept the safe, healthy love that was being given to me. It seemed foreign—and I was steadfast that something must be missing.

I remember saying to so many of my friends, my mother, and even Tay during one of our many "breaks" (insert Ross and Rachel joke here) that if I could only see myself the way that Tay saw me, I'd be all set. It was true. The way Tay saw me was the way I imagined my mother saw me—beaming with pride, the flaws that I see simply different colored roses in the rainbow garden. But you see, I couldn't see myself that way. I had healed the fear of abandonment (as much as one can heal a fear like that) when I went on my *Eat, Pray, #FML* trip. What I hadn't healed and fully figured out was how to love myself. Tay held up a mirror when he saw me in my purest form—and it scared the absolute shit out of me. It forced me to question if I was good enough. It forced me to realize how hard I had been on myself. It forced me to see myself through unjudgmental eyes. Simply put, it forced me to leave everything behind and truly go find myself—and for that type of healing, it is so incredibly worth taking the journey, whether you end up with the man holding the mirror or not.

If I hadn't gotten back to that pure form of self-love and if Tay hadn't learned that he was enough *without* someone else...*we would not have the type of strong relationship we have today.* Sometimes a love affair chews you up and spits you out—other times they are, in fact, your lobster. Don't make the mistake of confusing the two. People come into our lives for a purpose. Whether we attracted them for a reason, a season, or a lifetime...there is always a lesson waiting in the mirror if you're truly ready to look.

Taymour

I'd say it's a miracle that we made it here, but most of you who have read Gabrielle's two books already know that. This wasn't, and still isn't, your cookie-cutter kind of romance. There have been ups and downs, back-and-forths, lefts and rights, zigs and zags, and every detour in between. There've been mistakes and bad decisions but also the most honest and pure love I have ever felt. We have risen from whatever ash we had created in our lives, and together are forging the most beautiful future imaginable. And imagine it, I did. From our very first date, I visualized a future with her. As we grew, that visualization enhanced until it became a manifestation. I knew what I wanted, and she was it. She was my future. And you already know how it ends. But this is not about the outcome, this is about the journey. You know where we have made it to, and a lot of you know about the road we took to get there through her books. This is my side of our story.

It all started with a kiss...(record scratch)...oh wait. Wrong book. This one all started with a movie. Gabs and I met on a film set in Michigan. She was playing my younger sister in the movie. It was a fun little horror movie that unfortunately never saw the light of day. In fact, we never even finished filming the damn thing, as the funding ran out. But prior to that happening, we all had a blast and became fast friends. I remember the first time I met her. I knew she was the daughter of Dee Wallace, the living legend, but that was just about all I knew of her. I was going in blind. I did know one thing though; this girl was going to play my sister and we needed to have some of that familial chemistry. This is where Gabrielle likes to chime in and say that I'm a method actor and treat my roles fairly seriously, both of which are somewhat true. What is wholeheartedly true is that I, artistically, felt the need to bond with her more than any other person on that set and so bond we did.

We were fast friends that began acting like siblings in no time. My artistic need was being met, and I was making an incredible lifelong friend. Win-win. After day one, I kiddingly began calling her Peanut, as an older brother would do, which has stuck to this day. During the time of this film, I was engaged, and she was with her college boyfriend, who was actually there on location with us for a time. I state that because I think it is important for you to know that there was no chemistry between us...like in the least. We felt bonded on a soul level—not romantically. That came way later. Some ten years later, in fact. We really just clicked as friends and acted like siblings on that set. It was pure and fun until the plug got pulled on the film. Then we all went our merry ways. Gabrielle and I both lived in Los Angeles, but we never saw each other once after the film. Going on location to shoot a movie is weird in that you become a super close-knit family while making the movie and then the second people are back to reality, it all just becomes a memory. I'm not the first person to say that and definitely won't be the last.

We did stay in contact however and remained social-media close for the next ten years. It was ten years before I saw her again. And what a life lived within those ten years. I had married and had a child and gotten divorced. She was married and divorced and about to embark on her solo trip, which would eventually culminate in her first book. When she returned from that fateful trip, we planned on meeting up. She lays it out pretty epically in her second book, but there is no way she could write exactly how *my* heart felt and continues to feel every time I'm around her.

I believe it was some two months after her trip when we finally saw each other for the first time in a decade. At the time, I was bartending at a super exclusive bar in Hollywood called Adults Only. I found out she had been frequenting the place with her friends. This night she had planned on coming in a little early so we would have a chance to see each other. I remember being excited to see her, but I didn't anticipate anything more than that. I mean, it had been ten years.

Then she walked in. I was just floored. I knew she was beautiful, but there was something completely different about her beauty. I mean, she had been pretty ten years before, but the maturity gained in those ten years must've done something to her spirit and aura...and her face. She was fucking glowing, and it took me a minute to catch my breath. Still haven't caught it, by the way.

Once the night started going, I was busy and didn't get to spend much time with her, but the impression that she left on me that night was undeniable. I needed to see her again, but I needed to play my cards right. I didn't want to jeopardize our friendship over my budding feelings, so I tried to hold them in and just play it casual. About a week later, we went on our first date. According to her, it was definitely *not* a date, but it was. Not sure that qualifies as casual, but when I'm not around her, I get antsy. Another thing that hasn't gone away with time.

It was a quaint little French restaurant in the Valley called Bizou. Amazing reviews, amazing food, and fun crafty cocktails—and I didn't give a shit about any of it. I couldn't stop looking across the table at her. She was breathtaking to me in that moment—but as I soon learned, she is breathtaking in every moment. Another thing I soon learned is that she is the most kind, driven, ambitious, creative, confident, compassionate, helpful, loving person I have ever met. Just the bee's knees. There is nothing that can stop her, and that is infectious. This was a woman who at the time was broken, with her pieces all over the place. I caught her at her lowest—and thank God I did. To have had the privilege of watching her navigate all of the tribulations and come out as powerful as she is has been awe inspiring. She is my partner, yes, but moreover she is my foundation. She holds me up and creates that foundation for me so I can even have pillars. She is my everything. And to watch her grow and now raise our son only proves to me that she is that pot of gold at the end of the rainbow.

I knew after that dinner that she was *the one* (no, really, this time it's for real, I swear). I was ready...but was she? She still had a tremendous amount of healing to do from her heartbreak, and I needed to be compassionate about that. Those first few months were delicate and fun. We just watched movies and laughed, like all the fucking time. We still do. Something cosmic was happening inside of me. Something I hadn't felt in a long time. I was finally starting to feel relaxed in my life. I was constantly working on my health, my choices, and my career, all while showing up as the father my daughter deserved. To me, Gabrielle felt like the last piece of the puzzle. I was falling in love with her, and we hadn't even kissed yet. Well...that's never happened.

For those of you who have not read her two books, the second of which reflects on our journey, let me give you a quick synopsis. Gabrielle was married. Her husband had an affair with a nineteen-year-old. They divorced. Sometime later, she met a man she thought was the love of her life. He love bombed her into thinking she was the same. We will refer to him as Javier. I just threw up in my mouth a little. Okay, moving on. Anyway, after a whirlwind month-long romance, they profess their love for each other and decide to go to Europe together—yup, just puked again. Forty-eight-hours before they take off, he breaks it off with her, giving her some bullshit excuse. She, like the badass Phoenix that she is, decides to still go to Europe, solo. He still goes to Europe as well, solo. She writes her first book while on the trip. He continues to keep her on a roller coaster, sparking things up again, leaving her with even more confusion. She then comes back to the States.

Enter Tay.

We start dating, all the while still navigating her feelings for fuck-face, I mean Javier, as he continues to pull her along. It's a painful back-and-forth for the next two years, for everyone involved. She decides to take another soul-searching trip to Indonesia. She heals. She chooses herself, which, luckily, also means she chooses me. She completely ends it with Javier. She writes her second book, detailing that painful back-and-forth for two years, her journey to Indonesia, and finally our reunion. Okay. Do you need a shot of tequila? I do. I think that basically covered her two books, minus any detail whatsoever. Hopefully you get the gist. It really came down to me and Javier and which one of us was going to be lucky enough to share a life with Gabrielle.

It's easy to write about that back-and-forth now because I'm on the other side of it. But there wasn't a damn thing easy about it. There were a thousand and one lessons to be learned, and they needed to be learned quickly. Like I said earlier, I was unwavering in my intention and in my feelings for her. I saw my future, and it was clear for the very first time in my life. She checked every box. We waited a whole year to introduce her to my daughter and when they met, it was yet another check. Deep in my heart, I wasn't going anywhere. I was going to wait for her to choose me and if she didn't, I was going to jump off a cliff...just kidding. I would figure it out if it came to that.

It was during the back-and-forth times where the lesson of my life showed itself. My now mother-in-law took me to dinner and very simply told me exactly what I needed to hear. *I had to prove to myself that I could be happy being alone.* I had been going from relationship to relationship from the time my mother passed away. I had yet to be alone and be comfortable at the same time. It was crazy. The position Gabrielle was putting me in was exactly what I needed to progress in life. I just needed to accept it. We were mirroring our abandonment fears perfectly. It put everything into perspective for me. I soon began to shift my focus from her to me, trying to unlock any other wonderful little areas in myself that needed fixing. And just as I began to close those abandonment doors, Gabrielle began shifting her focus to me. Weird how the world works like that. Or is it?

I'm not going to lie. There were times within those two years that she made it extremely difficult for me to hold my focus on our future. It is very hard to hold on when you know they are with someone else...but hold on I did. I held on deep in my heart but now with the healthy feeling that I AM ENOUGH. I was able to walk through life with a smile.

And be okay being alone. Then, during one of the times we were broken up in that two-year span and after some time by myself, I was able to casually date without trying to fill that void.

It's a weird feeling when you know something is right, but they don't yet. You have to live your life kind of suspecting that they might never come around, so I did. I moved forward but with a serious hope that things would turn around. I was miserable without her. I so badly wanted what I knew we could get to—to where we are now. But I had to make sure she felt that as well. I had to give her the time to come to her own conclusion. I also believe she needed to see me healthy and alone, which she finally did.

Those were some extremely difficult times for me in other aspects as well. As explained in the addiction chapter, I was just coming out of an extremely tumultuous time in my life. I was well on my way to sobriety and healthiness but was still dealing with custody issues and now the potential pain of losing Gabrielle, so I was on a slippery slope to not fall into old habits. It was a sensitive and delicate time for me, and I needed to prevail. My life, my daughter's happiness, and my future with Gabrielle depended on it. *And so did the future of my soul.* It was all happening right then, and I needed to make the right choices.

And I did. Finally. I stayed clean. When life threw the kitchen sink at me, and a fourth and potentially fatal wave could be seen in the distance, I stayed clean. That was a huge win that I still reflect on today. Funny how the universe continues to give you chances to make the right choice, regardless of how many bad ones you have made in the past. Got to love the universe for that.

Perseverance got me through. Plain and simple. I look back at those two years and wonder how I made it. And yes, I really loved her, but there was something else at play. Something I couldn't put my finger on until much later. Now that we are some five to six years in, I can honestly say that through my perseverance I learned a great many things about my being. I learned that I am in fact a patient person, a trait that was never synonymous with my name. I learned that I am enough, just the way I am, as long as I continue to accept growth and change. I learned that just because someone says they need time, that does not mean that I am being abandoned. I learned that visualization and manifestation actually FUCKING WORKS. I learned that to make a future with someone, there has to be understanding and compassion and patience and true love. Not the shit you see in movies. Not the shit Javier was going to provide. It has to be absolutely real and cosmic at every turn. I learned that even in the best of relationships, you have to be willing to adjust and relearn and then adjust again. For so long, I went from relationship to relationship, yearning for that wild passion, those highs and lows that I witnessed in my parents. As beautiful as the good times were, there was always the other side. And that kind of back-and-forth or hot and cold began creating toxicity in the way I expected a relationship should be. That cycle and way of thinking needed to change.

Only after being with Gabrielle and working with her mom (in her healing practice) have I begun to shift that hardwired way of thinking. You learn by doing. Gabrielle and I have now spent the better part of six years as passionate and loving as you can imagine with only maybe a handful of arguments. Once I was able to find comfort in being alone and truly knowing that I was enough without Gabrielle—or anyone, for that matter—I ultimately filled that void myself. It was then, and only then, we found our way back to one another. If the relationship is the right one, you will never stop learning and growing and changing. Now, you just do it together. Is that not the broad definition of family?

Finding Home

"Every day is a journey, and the journey itself is home."
– Matsuo Bashō

It really is true that everything happens for a reason. Not in the toxic positivity way, where people walk around smiling like rainbows are coming out of their assholes, pretending that the grenades life throws at you aren't fucking devastating at times. But when you look for the triggers, lessons, the deeper meanings, and the ways to grow and evolve—*therein lies the reason.*

We decided to write this chapter together, because that is how our story ended—*together.* Whether you picked up this book to figure out why you haven't been able to find the relationship you desire or you need to somehow fix or leave the one you're in, or even if you just wanted an entertaining, thought-provoking way to meet yourself a little deeper, we hope you found something that you didn't have when you started.

From the very beginning of both our lives we were challenged to take on the healing of abandonment. Only once we realized that was the task at hand did we fully understand what an undertaking it would be. To heal a wound that spans many circumstances and most likely many lifetimes is a challenge filled with lessons and reasons—*if* you're willing to find and learn from them.

For both of us, the loss of our respective parents gave us very clear beliefs at a wildly young age: *When I love someone, they leave* and *I am not enough.*

How can you find the reasons in losing such an important figure so young? If Gabrielle had not experienced that type of loss to begin with, she wouldn't have been left with the subconscious belief that would create so many important experiences in her life, ultimately leading her to a transformative journey that resulted in a book that has helped so many people around the world. She would not have witnessed firsthand what it looks like to overcome and heal, through watching her incomparable mother handle losing the love of her life with grace. And she would have not come to have the peace around death she now has—no matter how unfair or untimely it may seem.

When Taymour lost his mother, he decided how he would live his life—like there is no tomorrow. He would hug tighter, sit in the moments a little longer, and love just a little bit deeper. He began his journey to learn to process grief as it comes and to realize that there is something to be said for sitting in it when you need to. Whether through a random kiss in the European rain or waiting for the love of your life to finally make the right decision, you will always come out the other side of it.

Without the experience of that first love and that first big heartbreak, neither of us would have fully understood how deep that void was within ourselves. That hole we were both actively seeking to patch. That scar our parents left on our hearts...it was so beautifully demonstrated by those early relationships.

Gabrielle would not have come to know so surely that we do go on after this life, in this body—a comfort that has carried her through many devastating lows. She would not have understood, as an adult, how absolutely fleeting life can be—and how we should cherish our relationships as if every day is our last.

For Tay, his first love showed him how it felt when that void was temporarily filled, sending him through relationship after relationship on a quest to find that again. Each one taught him to let go of patterns he witnessed growing up and, most importantly, showed him that he didn't believe he was enough on his own.

Our individual and very different battles with addiction brought us more lessons and reasons than we can count. The most important is that addiction comes from within, hiding dormant in your system from past traumas that have been swept aside, waiting to be healed. It is often used as a Band-Aid or patch for something deep that is screaming to be attended to. Tay's multiple waves of substance abuse tried to vigorously pull him into its dark current—only to bring the unresolved grief he had been swimming away from for decades to the surface. He had been treading water for years as the grief sat just underneath the dark waters below. Finally, he stopped kicking, sank down, and allowed himself to almost drown in it all. Only then was he able to see what the addiction was attempting to numb, decide to intentionally feel it, and just in time, grab thirteen-year-old Tay and swim back up to the surface to breathe.

Gabrielle's addiction has given her the gift of knowing that she is in control and always has a choice. It has allowed her to go on a journey with her body and come to a place of peace and respect in regards to it. But most importantly, it has allowed her to step into her power, knowing that she can make the choice to let go and heal. That a mistake or a moment does not have to define you—and that the right people will hold space for you to continue to make those mistakes and hold your hand through it.

The friendships we have both experienced in this life, some that have withstood the test of time and others that served their purpose and have since faded away, have shaped who we are today. Gabrielle's early experience in choosing herself would inevitably guide her to leaving an unhealthy marriage—and closing the chapter on a friendship that had turned toxic. And Tay learned that, sometimes, people *do* stay. These friendships have lifted us up, dusted us off, and allowed us to find a life raft in the often chaotic waters that we call life.

Divorce is never fun, whether you are taking your life back after cheating or learning the hard lesson that sometimes the healthier choice for everyone is to simply leave. Our first marriages taught us so many things, and even though our individual experiences were drastically different, neither of us can imagine not having had them. Gabrielle felt proud for choosing herself and once again saw how life cannot break you but empowers you. That ultimately led her to fulfill such an important part of her life—because you can't get to the heartbreak, European adventure, and all the healing without the asshole who cheated on you first. Tay finally recognized that the right relationship shouldn't be dramatic or chaotic like his parents were growing up. That love can be safe, healthy, passionate, wonderful, and boring all at the same time. We both needed to learn that lesson, and we're so incredibly grateful for the relationships that helped us get there.

Triggers are here to teach us about ourselves and remind us what little bits of ourselves still need a little love and healing, almost as if we have a little conductor inside of our hearts who stabs us with his stupid little baton to get us to wake up and pay attention. They can shape us, hinder us, heal us, or be the death of us. It is up to us to take responsibility and decide how we navigate them—and to allow those close to us a peek behind the curtain so they can hold our hand along the way. Find those people. Share your triggers with them. Allow them to not only be a mirror but a support in working through them. And always remember:

Relationships are mirrors.

Mirrors show you triggers.

Choose to heal.

Children will always be one of the greatest sources of healing, partly because, for so many of us, they are our love place. It is hard to find something as heart opening as your child's giggle or their small hand wrapped in yours. And partly because their soul has chosen you, not only for the lessons they have come to learn, but to help you heal yourself. Just when you think you've done the work, watch what happens when a child makes their grand entrance. Hello, old wounds; hello, buried trauma; hello, all the stuff we thought we had worked through. What a gift to be able to heal through the innocent eyes of your child. What a gift to be able to teach all the lessons, share all the wisdom, and protect them from the things we have already learned in this life. But mostly, what a gift to have someone who loves us so greatly and unconditionally that we are able to stumble through life, make mistakes, and learn and grow all over again with them.

With all these small lessons and reasons for the traumas, experiences, highs and lows, there is one thing that bears mention more than the rest. These things, these memories, these paths we've walked down—*is what made us into the people we are today.* Without the times you've cried on the floor, broken and bruised, feeling as if you're surrounded by all-encompassing darkness, you would not be able to recognize the bright and blinding light. We are humans. Humans who have intense experiences that shape and mold us into diverse, complicated, fascinating individuals. Our experiences make up our spiritual DNA. They leave emotional memories on a once-blank canvas. What a privilege it is to look at a person toward the end of their life and see a story truly worth reading. Tales in every imprinted wrinkle. Adventures in each scar. Emotions in every blink. This is life. It is what it means to be alive. It is what we live and breathe for as humans. And sometimes it is painful. But if you can find the beauty hidden within that pain—and we promise you, it is there—then it will not feel as if it happened for nothing but as if it was part of the intricate stitch line that holds you together and makes you...*you.*

We found each other at a few different times in our lives. Our paths first crossed when we were both in relationships and had so much more to do before we were ready to meet as partners. After ten years of experiences, mistakes, lessons, relationships, children, divorces, and heartbreaks, we found each other again—this time, as mirrors for each other. It was our choice to pay attention to all the triggers in the mirror and decide to heal them. *Only then* did we find ourselves in a happy, healthy, life-affirming love that we hold onto so dearly—because we truly know and appreciate how precious it is.

What is meant for you will always find you if you do the work and choose to heal yourself—whether it takes a few months, a few years, or ten. Life is so much more than any one experience or relationship. It is all of those experiences, the deaths, the tragedies, the miracles, the great loves, and all the lessons they bring. *That is a life worth living.*

So if you're wandering through life, trying to figure out where your person is, there is a good chance you have not yet become the person *you* need to be to meet them. And if you're in a relationship searching for the spark that is nowhere to be found—it *can* be reignited. The answers—whether good, bad, ugly, or hard to accept—*are always within yourself.* Search for them. Sit with them. Hear them. Invite them to have tea with you.

How could Tay ever find the love he so desperately wanted if he had not yet trained his spirit that it is okay to be alone, allowing him to undoubtedly know that he was, in fact, enough.

How could Gabrielle accept a love that would never abandon her if she never truly realized she would never abandon herself?

Us finding each other didn't happen by chance. It didn't happen by luck. It didn't even happen by fate. We did the work. We learned the lessons. We searched for the answers and sat with them once we found them. We took the journeys. Because only then, when two people truly have gone on their journeys, can they say:

I found you through finding me.

Gabrielle

The biggest thank you to everyone who has been a part of our journey, big or small, that was written about in this book. Erica, our amazing editor turned friend, for talking us off the edge more than a few times. My mother, who has shown me what it means to never give up. All of my FMLers, who have been on this journey with me from the very beginning. Kristofer and Haley, for reminding me that main characters sometimes show up later on in your life, and are very much worth the wait. My dad, Christopher, who will always live in my heart. My step-dad, Skip—thank you for showing me how important it is to be a step-parent. And for anyone that made it to this part of the book...I thank you and acknowledge the journey you've just taken to get here.

Taymour

I am forever grateful to my family, who have stuck by me through all of it. My father and my brother, who have guided the ship. My co-parent, Katy, and all my friends, who continue to support the ship. My pillars, Aunt Elaine and Mama Dee Wallace, without whom I would not be here.

My wife and my children, for whom my future is laid.